Endorsements

Story telling is Gods chosen way to communicate with us. This book is no exception. As he navigates the twists and turns of Gods fluid plan, Warwick tells a remarkable story of God's direction, God's correction, God's guidance and sometimes God's silence. As you come to know Warwick and June through the telling of their story, I hope that you, as a reader, will be as captivated and challenged as I have been while reading this stirring tale. It is amazing what God can do through two lives, well lived, and well "gived".

Tom Bremer
Director, Europe Teen Challenge
President, ISAAC International.

Great book Warwick and June to see the path that God has led you both and your family in the world of drug, alcohol and porn addiction, prisons, homelessness and rehabilitation and restoration that leads to transformation. There is an amazing degree of pain and heartache that you have witnessed and walked through that is enough to tear ones heart out but at the same time of stories of redemption and transformation which are amazing and life changing. Thanks for not quitting in this fight. We have had the privilege of walking with you in this world in Europe, Asia and Australia and you are some of our heroes. Thank you for you love for people, for God and your practical service to some of the most vulnerable people that others have given up on. This book shows, the good, the bad and the ugly and what happens when a spiritual Mum and Dad are set loose to get to know God and to serve His purposes in this broken world. This is what the Gospel looks like and be careful as you read the Murphy story, it will move you to action.

Steve and Marie Goode
Authors 'Bring Your Eyes and See – Our Journey into Justice, Compassion and Action'
YWAM Champions of Mercy, Justice and Action.
Bangkok, Thailand

Marti and I have known Warwick and June Murphy for nearly five decades. I commend them warmly, and through this book you will feel you know them as well, and that is a privilege. Their adventure of being redeemed by God's loving-kindness and mercy, and then obeying the leading of the Holy Spirit, is another episode in the huge history of God at work in the lives of individuals. Very exciting!

Lynn Green
YWAM Elder, Harpenden, United Kingdom

This book is a heartfelt testimony to the power of joy. It opens up with glimpses from the life of a boy maverick turned into a religious and social rebel. A life that on a personal and family scale brushed too painfully with the tragedies of alcoholism and addiction, only to be then led the challenges facing seekers of the true Spirit of Christ in churches and organizations struggling with traditionalism and hypocrisy. From there, unto the glory that only those who witness firsthand what the Spirit can do in transforming the despair and brokenness in the lives of hard core addicts, changing them into the abundance of a beaming life full of gratitude, courage, service and true freedom. The powerful ministry of the mature June and Warwick Murphy, has touched multitudes in almost every country in Asia, and this adventurous reading will leave you with a taste of the joy, audacious hope and unadulterated faith of the humble but truly great couple; June and Warwick Murphy.

Dr. Ehab El Kharrat
Founder and director of the Freedom Drugs and HIV programme in Egypt
Former president of ISAAC

Having had the privilege of getting to know Warwick and June through the ISAAC network, it was great to read this book and understand more of how God has led them in their ministry. Their story is one of challenge, heartache and joy, all told with self deprecating humour. Their friendship, wisdom and hospitality have benefitted so many people, me included, and this book provides more opportunities for others to learn from their wealth of experience – and perhaps embark on their own "adventure like no other' with God.

Treflyn Lloyd-Roberts,
ISAAC International General Secretary.
Chief Executive Yeldall Christian Centres

What a delightful, human-reassuring adventure to experience with Warwick as he takes us into the many "on the ground" ways God deals with him, and thus also with us, who seek to follow Him in flesh and in faith. Talking is cheap but in these life stories Warwick and June have sown and cultivated a garden of lessons in faith that inspire and make us smile, in nods or rolling eyes….as the flowers and fruits of their journeys refresh and nourish our belief in a personal and loving God. What a wonderful God indeed!

Pastor Pax Tan (Lutheran and Baptist)
Former Senior Director, Malaysian CARE
Certified Substance Abuse Counsellor and Trainer
Vice-President, International Substance Abuse and Addiction Coalition (ISAAC International)

An

ADVENTURE LIKE NO OTHER

Discovering that God's Classroom Has No Walls

By
WARWICK MURPHY

VIDE

Copyright © 2021 by Vide Press

Vide Press and The Christian Post are not responsible for the writings, views, or other public expressions by the contributors inside of this book, and also any other public views or other public content written or expressed by the contributors outside of this book. The scanning, uploading, distribution of this book without permission is theft of the Copyright holder and of the contributors published in this book. Thank you for the support of our Copyright.

Vide Press
6200 Second Street
Washington D.C. 20011
www.VidePress.com

ISBN: 978-1-954618-04-6
ISBN: 978-1-954618-05-3

Printed in the United States of America

Cover designed by MiblArt.com

Psalm 71:17-19.

O God, you have taught me from my youth;
And I still declare thy wondrous deeds.
And even when I am old and grey, O God, do not forsake me,
Until I declare Thy strength to this generation,
Thy power to all who are to come.
For Thy Righteousness, O God, reaches to the heavens,
Thou hast done great things;
O God, who is like You?

Dedication

I want to dedicate this book to my family, who have walked so much of this road with me. Firstly, to my wife, June. She has supported me, encouraged me, challenged me and put up with me and I am so grateful to her for loving me.

To my children, who are all adults and parents themselves now. In many ways, you did not have much choice in this, and I am aware that there were many times when you would have wished that we had been living a 'normal life'. I hope that you can look back now and see many things that have been beneficial through this strange road that we, as a family, have walked down.

To the four people who have married into our family. Thank you for being prepared to learn and understand what makes this family somewhat different from anything else you may have known, or expected.

Finally, to my grandchildren. This book was initially written for you. So that you would know something of the history, and the reasons, why we have not always been there for you. We too have missed the times we would have loved to spend with you, but we believe that the legacy we leave behind is of more importance. Obedience to the leading of God we believe is one of the greatest lessons anyone can learn. In the book of Matthew, we are told that after Jesus sent his disciples out to minister, He then went and ministered to their families. We hope that you know that the arms of a loving God surround you at all times, even when you don't feel them there.

Introduction

I shut the door for the last time, walked down the steps to the front gate, turned and took one last look at the house that had been our home and ministry center for over eight years. The building was just another typical London house, three floors up and one floor down. It looked like most of the other houses on the street but the stories that it carried of changed lives made it a very special house indeed.

The emotion of leaving for the last time was overwhelming. The faces and names of so many who had found peace in this house came flooding back. Former residents such as Mikey, Dave, Del, Gerry, Keith, Dele, and so many more. The staff who had worked with us: Sue, Heidi, Martin, Steve, Stoney, and Bridget. Memories of the good times and the bad times raced through my mind as I shut the gate and drove off.

Beth Shalom was a residential rehabilitation facility situated just south of the river in London. Residents entered into a 12-month program aiming to overcome their problems with drugs or alcohol.

My wife, June, and I had established this centre and been the directors since we opened the doors in 1983. We lived on site and raised our family in that house. In fact, to quote Dale Kerrigan from the movie, *The Castle*, *"it was not a house, it was indeed a home"* for our family, and for those who passed through.

The church has often been accused of not caring, of being too heavenly minded to be of any earthly use. Well, Beth Shalom was a wonderful example of the Gospel in action. Hurting people were not only cared for, but they were also drawn into relationships they never knew could exist. They grew in their confidence, they stopped using drugs, and they began walking a new pathway with new friends and a clean heart.

This book is about how all this happened, about the story of a boy from Sydney, Australia. At least that is how it started out. As I have been writing, it has become apparent that this book is actually about God. About the leading of God in the lives of ordinary people. It is about lessons of faith. It is indeed about the fact that God is eternally faithful and true to His character, and that living in His Kingdom is learning to place our total dependence on Him.

One of the problems in writing a book such as this is that there is a temptation, much like there is with a newsletter, to make everything sound like it is positive and rosy and that great things have been achieved. While great things may have been achieved, it is important to state that every day was not a bed of roses. Living a life of trusting God for finances, and working in the addictions field, has good days and not so good days. I want to try to make sure that we tell the whole truth in this book.

The journey of adventure in this book occurred in three phases, so I have set out the book in those phases. As is usual in life, those phases, although clear in their content, still merge from one to the other as you will see. Each phase deals with different periods of my life and each phase talks about the impact and involvement that three different organizations have had on my life. The Salvation Army, Youth With a Mission (YWAM), and ISAAC (International Substance Abuse and Addiction Coalition).

PHASE 1

An Adventure takes you to unknown places

Chapter 1
First Steps

How did we ever get into a world of heroin, prison visits, street people, and misery? This is a question often asked of my wife, June, and myself. Working with drug users, prostitutes, and people with sexual identity problems is not the sort of career choice you make when you leave school. It certainly was not the career choice I had made.

June and I are Australians. I was raised in Sydney. The youngest of three children. June grew up in Melbourne. The only daughter with two brothers.

I had a dream similar to most Australian young people at that time. To get a good job, get married, build a house on a quarter-acre block, and live the Australian dream. When I left school, I did an apprenticeship as a pastry cook. I had no concept of where I would end up. The truth is, I was immature and living a life focused on what was happening "today" with no real thought for the future. A few years after finishing my apprenticeship and a broken relationship, I left home in Sydney to follow that other dream of many Australians: to travel around this vast continent. Most Australians, even though we might like to think we are Crocodile Dundee, actually live on the coastal fringes of the continent. Somewhere along the line this dream of travelling around Australia grew into something that should be done by everyone. For most people, they wake from the dream and get on with other things. However, for me and one of my friends, Neil, we thought we could make this dream come true. To this end we had been working on restoring an old VW Kombi van which we were going to use for this trip. The dream was to get work in different places and see Australia. As this dream eventually died the Kombi Van never did get restored. My friend suddenly left Sydney on his own and a few months later I packed up my car and began my own adventure. I got as far as Melbourne before my life changed forever.

I had gone to Melbourne as my first stop, because one of my brothers and his family were living there and I figured I would get free board. However, my Kombi friend had moved to Melbourne some time earlier and he was, by this time, living in a Christian community up in the hills outside Melbourne. How had he become involved with this church? I had no idea, but it should have rung some alarm bells for me.

He was doing a three-month Bible Discipleship program run by the church he was attending. I should mention that he had a history of looking into other religions which is why alarm bells should have been heard. After all, it was the '70s and there was a new guru on every street corner telling us that they held the key to 'the truth', whatever that was. At one stage I recall he carried a photo of an Indian guru called Meha Baba in his wallet and would quite happily engage people in discussion about religion. Neil had written to me about his involvement with this church in Melbourne, so I was not surprised to find him doing this course. He told me that he only had a week to go before the training course finished and I would be welcome as a guest for that week. So, I headed to the hills without any idea that the whole course of my life was about to change.

Chapter 2

Foundations

I need to give some background here that may be helpful to the reader. The family I grew up with consisted of my parents, two older brothers, and myself. Dad went out to work and mum did some part time work at home. Very typical of the time. It was the '50s. Australians, like people in much of the world, were looking at rebuilding after the Second World War. The focus for most was "put your head down, work hard, and make a life for your family". As I look back probably one of the key things about our family was that we were part of the Salvation Army in Sydney. My grandparents, on Dad's side, had been Salvationists and my parents were as well. This meant that on Sundays my brothers and I would put on our little suits, with short pants I might add, and attend the "meetings" (they were not called services in the Sallies), three times each Sunday. Having to be at the morning meeting, the Sunday School in the afternoon, and then the evening meeting each week meant that Sundays were quite full. As a young boy it also meant learning to play a brass instrument, beginning with a cornet, and moving on to the trombone later. Sundays were meant to be a day of rest, a day supposedly to focus on God. According to my grandmother, this meant no boisterous games outside, no entertainment, etc., although it seems to have been OK for my mum to stay home in the mornings so that she could prepare the usual Sunday roast dinner, with dessert. My father figured it was not a meal if there was no dessert, and mum could make some wonderful desserts. She did this in a house with a corrugated iron roof which, in summer in Sydney, was like an oven itself. So, the meetings were in fact a relief for a young boy as the building was made of brick which made things a bit cooler. This style of Christianity was all that I knew. Hymns sung from a hymnbook accompanied by a brass band. Someone preaching, not too long mind you! Sunday school and other activities that the Army ran from time to time. In short, a very conservative style of Christianity, especially compared to what is presented today. This helps explain what happened in Melbourne. I was raised in the Salvation Army and still today I get a thrill to hear a Salvation Army band playing. I am still in touch with many friends from the Salvation Army. So many of these people were a great influence in my life and were, and are, good friends. The values I was exposed to through the days of my youth were deeply embedded within me. They were a source of annoyance to me as I tried to live a very different life, but they would also bear fruit many years later. The values and foundations we build into the lives of our children are rarely wasted.

Although I have described the Salvation Army meetings as "conservative" let's not forget that historically they were a radical movement of people who had a message to share and would find whatever method that they believed would bring people to listen to that message. The Salvation Army was founded in 1865 in the east end of London. When William Booth, the founder of the Salvation Army, preached he would preach to thousands at a time, without a microphone, but still able to hold the audience spellbound. They introduced the brass band, the military style uniform, and their leaders were called officers, not reverends. In the Salvation Army, people do not put money into an offering plate. They "fire their cartridge" instead. The buildings where they hold their meetings are not called churches, they are called Citadels, or Corps to stick with the military thinking. It was not uncommon to hear someone call out, during the meeting, **"Fire a volley,"** and the response from the congregation was **"Amen."** They took their message to the streets and endured persecution in the process. They took their message to

Chapter 2 Foundations

those they believed were most in need. William Booth's call was to **"go for souls and go for the worst"**, and that is what they did.

The impact that the Salvation Army had on Britain in those early years was powerful. These early Salvationists were brave people indeed. Ridicule and abuse were expected every time they ventured onto the street. In fact, the opposition to this new movement became so organised that they named themselves the Skeleton Army, as though they came from the pit of hell. These were not just a group of hecklers, they were a violent, vicious body of people who physically attacked the Salvation Army soldiers.

The commitment of these Salvationists was not to be questioned, and as they continued to reach out to the poor and needy in the slums of those great cities in Victorian Britain the abuse turned to respect. When William Booth died in August, 1912, his coffin was carried through the streets of London and crowds in their thousands lined the streets to mourn the passing of a prophet who had shown them compassion and care in their need. He had also challenged the very fabric of a society that had allowed such poverty and need to be seen as normal. It needs to be added here that William Booth probably would not have achieved what he did without the encouragement and wisdom of his partner and wife, Catherine Booth, who was a formidable evangelist in her own right. I would encourage anyone to read further on those early days of the Salvation Army to see what one couple, sold out to a caring God, can achieve in their lifetime.

However, as times moved on the organization changed, like most organizations. As a young boy, I was able to see some of the changes. My grandparents had become Christians under the ministry of William Booth in England many years back. But I can still remember my grandmother, and others of her generation, being quite vocal in the meetings. It was not uncommon to hear people of that generation shouting out *"Hallelujah"* and *"Praise the Lord"* as the officer was preaching. They were used to a meeting being a very lively affair, but things were changing by the time I was on the scene. It seemed to me that what had been used to draw people to the meetings in the past had now become more of a formality. The process seemed to become more important than the message. One particular incident may help readers to understand what I am saying.

Every Sunday morning the band and the officers would go to different places to hold what was called an "open-air meeting". They would be at hospitals, nursing homes, or maybe just on a street corner in a suburb nearby. On Sunday evenings we also held an open-air meeting. This meeting was always in the same place, on a side street in a shopping center, not far from the Salvation Army Citadel in North Sydney. When they had first started holding open-air meetings there many years previously, this spot had been a very busy place with lots of people passing by. However, all these years later, shops were closed in Australia on Sundays. There was no one passing by anymore. Yet we would faithfully gather there each Sunday evening at 6pm. We would form up in a semicircle and the band would play. Someone would read some scripture. Someone would share a testimony of what God was doing in their life and someone would preach a short message. Then we would reform into ranks and march back to the Citadel, through a major intersection with the band playing some stirring march music. This process was all very good, but the fact that there was hardly anyone listening to what we were doing seemed to have escaped our notice. As a young man, I wondered what purpose there was to this. So, on the way to the open-air meeting one Sunday night, I asked one of the older bandsmen why we did this when there was often no one listening. I have never forgotten his reply. He looked at me somewhat surprised by my question, and said, *"Because we have always done it."*

Thankfully, I am aware that the Salvation Army has indeed tried to change with the times in recent days. And sadly, as is often the case when things need to change there are those who struggle to understand why. My father was one of them. He was

Chapter 2 Foundations

totally committed to the Army but could not come to terms with the changes that were taking place, even when they were small changes. I recall an occasion when we were visiting my parents and, on Sunday, we all went to the Army together. Dad had retired from playing in the band by this stage as his eyesight and other facets of his health were failing. The first hymn was accompanied by the band and we all rose to sing together. Later in the meeting, the band moved aside to allow a few people with guitars and a drum set to lead the next song. Everyone else in the meeting was standing to sing, except my dad. I would have laughed, if it had not been so sad. When we arrived home, he was still complaining about the use of guitars and "why do we need such things?"

I need to state here that these were my perceptions, and one thing I have learned as a counsellor is that a person's perceptions are not always correct. The faith and belief of the people I grew up with in the Salvation Army is not in question. It was my behavior and beliefs that were in question. Many of those people impacted my life far more than they will ever know and I am thankful for their input into my life.

Chapter 3

Poor Choices

When I got my driving licence, first motorbike, and then my first car, life changed. I now had freedom to go where I wanted, and I did. There were things on offer that I could now access without having to let someone else know where I was. I was keen to engage in this life and jumped in as much as I could while still putting on my uniform on Sundays and playing in the band. I was trying to live two lives at the same time. This of course could not continue without ending in pain. One night in particular brought my double life to an end.

I had been with some friends in Kings Cross, a notorious part of Sydney. Kings Cross was, and still is, the sleazy nightclub area of Sydney. Strip clubs, drugs on offer, prostitutes plying their business, and, at that time, large numbers of US soldiers on leave from service in Vietnam. My friends and I were celebrating a birthday and we ended up in Kings Cross that night. I was already developing a taste for alcohol and on this night had drunk far too much. In my inebriated state I mouthed off to a passing police officer. Not the smartest thing to do, and in a very short time I found myself in the back of a police Paddy Wagon with a whole bunch of old winos. We were taken to the nearest police station, which happened to have been part of an old prison built in the convict days in Sydney. I was marched up to the desk where a sergeant took down my details. One question was, **"What religion**

Chapter 3 Poor Choices

are you?" I hesitated before saying, *"Salvation Army"*. For the first time in this interview he looked up at me, shook his head and said, *"You should be ashamed of yourself."* Which I was. I was then taken to a cell, which was already crowded with the Saturday night regulars. Drunks and winos who all knew the drill. There were only so many blankets available and they had them all. Having mouthed off to a police officer already, I was not about to make things worse by arguing with some belligerent drunk in a confined space. There was one other guy who, like me, had found himself in a place he had never intended to be on that Saturday night. We had both sobered up quite quickly and sat there telling each other why we should not be in that position. The stench in the cell from the regulars was overpowering to say the least. After four hours I was released with a warning. I stepped out of the police station having no idea how to get home only to find my mates, also Salvationists, but not drinkers, were waiting outside for me. They drove me back to one of their places and threw me into the bath, trying to get rid of the smell which it seemed had penetrated even my skin and was oozing out of every pore.

By now, of course, it was early Sunday morning. I was trying to tell my mates that I could not go to the Army in my condition. They told me I had to go. So, I did. It was a morning at the Army to forget. I was sure I still reeked from my time in the cells. I could not concentrate on the music and could see my mates all having a laugh at my expense. The results of that night would play out over the next week.

In the Salvation Army, if a person is found to be behaving in a manner that goes against regulations then you will be "stood down." Later that week, the Officer called to let me know that I was being stood down from duty. He said I would not be allowed to play in the band or participate in Salvation Army activities for a period of weeks. However, I could still attend the meetings and wear the uniform. The idea behind this of course is that the person will use the time to consider their poor behavior before God and decide to change their ways for the better. This whole process was humbling and embarrassing to say the least. I tried to make light of it of course. Isn't that what arrogant young people do? Putting on a "front" while dying inside.

It was the situation that caused me to choose which life I wanted. In the words of the old knight in the Indiana Jones movie, ***"I chose poorly."*** I decided that my trombone playing days were over, probably making life easier for the bandmaster I would think.

So, I had a foundation of conservative Christianity and a taste for something wilder in life. Yet, amongst all of this, I was just another confused young man trying to make sense of a crazy world. Did I believe in God? Certainly, and herein lay my big dilemma, because the life I was now living was far away from Him and I had a constant fear that if I died in that state I would not be in heaven. I would be lost forever. The foundations of belief we build in a child's life never actually leave them. They lay there like a bedrock in that life. In some, they go on to build solid structures on those foundations. For others, the foundations get covered over with other things, but if an archaeologist were to dig into that life, they would still find those foundations sitting under all the other beliefs in that person's life. Those years, and my lifestyle, proved to be very costly financially. I look back on the number of car accidents I had while under the influence and I am very grateful for praying parents.

Chapter 4
Life Changing Decision

So here I was, a guest at a Bible college in the hills on the outskirts of Melbourne. In my mind I was on the first leg of a journey around Australia. I was still looking for more of the so-called "good times" in life. I believed that with my upbringing in the Salvation Army I could behave myself for a week with all these Bible college students. I knew how to present a good façade after all.

My friend, Neil, had not told me much about the church or the training course that he was involved in, so I assumed that I would meet a bunch of people studying the Bible with a few songs thrown in. As it happened, I was the one thrown into the deep end of something I had no knowledge of at all.

The first morning I was there, we all met in the large lounge room for "worship." We stood in a circle, someone was playing a guitar and they started singing songs I had never heard. As they sang, people started raising their hands in the air while their eyes were closed. That morning there was no chance that my eyes were closing. The next thing I was aware of was the people near me were speaking words that I could not understand and seemed to have no connection to any language that I had heard before. I came to learn that they were "speaking in tongues." By this stage I was totally convinced that my friend had managed to get himself involved with some weird cult and I was determined to make sure that I did not get involved, but I had told Neil that I would stay for the week and I was keen to spend time with him. However, as the week progressed, more shocks were in store for me. On Sunday we traveled to a hall where the whole church gathered. I was at first surprised by the number of people. There would have been upwards of 500 people gathered there. Then I was surprised by the style of worship. Then the preaching, and finally, an altar call. All common terms to me now, but back then it was all glaringly new. This was my introduction to Pentecostal/Charismatic Christianity.

Two other things happened during that week that led to changes in my life. The first was seeing one of the girls at the training course who caught my eye. She was outgoing, easy to talk to, and I was always a sucker for a pretty face. This girl eventually became my wife. More on that later. The second thing was that the people I met at the church and the training course were all quite intelligent and "normal." The thing that made them different was a faith in God that I had only come across in the lives of a few people during my life.

I find it interesting that in most cases when Christians are depicted in movies and TV shows they are often shown as bigoted, unintelligent, or busybodies wanting to poke their noses in where they are not wanted. The truth is quite different of course. Christians run businesses, they send their children to local schools, they are involved in local sporting clubs. In short, they are not that different to anyone else, apart from what actually drives their lives. These people were actually trying to live out their walk with God and seeing exciting things as a result. They were believing what the Bible had to say with regards to every area of their lives. Relationships, finance, family, and reaching out to those in need. All of this was confronting to someone who thought he was simply on the first leg of a great adventure

Chapter 4 Life Changing Decision

traveling around Australia. When I look back, I can see that the adventure I had in mind was quite small compared to the adventure that God had planned for me.

Even though I had grown up going to church every Sunday and had heard the Gospel message numerous times, my life was a long way from being that of a Christian's. I had stopped wearing the Sally uniform some years back and was living a life of as many "good times" as I could find. For some years I had been developing a drinking habit that was growing worse as time went on. My drinking had become so problematic that I missed voting in one election because I had passed out in a toilet cubicle of the pub where I was a regular. Looking back now I have no doubt that if I had continued, I would have become a chronic alcoholic with all that that entails. Both my brothers' lives were heavily affected by alcohol and all the pain that goes with that for their families. But, like most problem drinkers, I thought I was in control. Why? Because I was measuring myself against the people I was drinking with, and they didn't have a problem, did they? Or so I fooled myself into believing at the time. This is the illogical thinking that alcoholics and addicts fool themselves with. I had also been dabbling in the drug scene during this time, and, like most young men, I was finding the opposite sex to be a great focus of my attention. I had left Sydney to escape from the pain of a broken relationship, which was probably a very wise decision by the girl ending the relationship with me. Now here I was in Melbourne at a Bible school being confronted with the choice to either accept the reality of God's claim on my life or continue down what I now know to be a road of self-destruction. Did I understand that the road I was on led to destruction? Yes, but like most people on that road we believe that we will be the ones that have a different outcome. Terrible things happen to other people, not us. In truth we lie to ourselves because the truth raises all manner of questions in us. Like, why am I behaving this way when it goes against everything I have been taught? What is it that drives me to continue in this way?

AN ADVENTURE LIKE NO OTHER | *Warwick Murphy*

The impact of that week at the Bible school, and church, was enormous. Listening to and watching the people from that church showed me very clearly that real Christianity was very different to what I had been believing. The adventure I had in mind was about to come to an end, but the adventure God had in mind was just beginning.

At the end of my week as a guest at the Bible School, I sat in my car one morning and said to God that, if I became an actual believing Christian, then I wanted it to be real. I did not want to just sit on a pew on Sundays. I wanted to give my life into His hands and serve Him. That morning, I committed my life to God not knowing where that would take me. At the time I had no concept of how deeply God takes us at our word when our hearts are being real with Him. I now know that God takes us at our word, and He did. Very quickly in fact.

In many ways this was a very unemotional decision. To my mind I had come to a very clear fork in the road. Clearly the sensible thing to do was follow Christ. I had little understanding of how my sin had affected God. I had little understanding of the price that Jesus paid. It still amazes me that I could have heard the Gospel message so often and yet not heard it at all. Even though I had heard the story of God's incarnation and I knew the basics of what Easter is about, I had never spent any time considering that God suffered for my behavior. That Jesus went through indescribable agony just for me. I had no understanding that Jesus did all that because God is love, and that, because He is love, His every thought and action towards me were actions of love. I have since realised that it is not good enough to just be a Christian to get a ticket to heaven. I should live my life following the example of Jesus as an act of obedience to the One who loves me. My activities actually touch the heart of God, giving Him joy or pain. And so, a whole new life, a whole new world, opened up to me that morning. My decision that morning to give my life over to God ended the adventure I had in mind for myself and began the adventure that God had in mind for me. An adventure like no other.

Chapter 5

Go, or Stay?

One of the leaders in this church was a former Salvation Army Officer named Tony Fitzgerald. Tony was an evangelist and led a team of people, from the church, who were reaching out to the street people, the drug dealers, the prostitutes, and drinkers who were to be found in the suburb of St Kilda in Melbourne. They were based in a shop front on the main street that ran through this area. St Kilda is an inner-city suburb of Melbourne. At the time, this was the seedy part of Melbourne. The drug dealing and using, the prostitution, the cheap nightclubs, etc. Most cities have such a place. I quickly joined Tony's team and felt excited and somehow comfortable in this work. But like most street ministries, I learned more about myself here than I did about anyone else. I recall one of the regulars to the coffee shop, a young homosexual guy who really liked to present as effeminate. He very soon worked out that I was extremely uncomfortable being around him. I was fine with everyone else, but his behaviour confronted all my "macho Aussie bloke" attitudes I had inside me. Needless to say, every time he came into the coffee shop, he made a beeline for me and enjoyed sidling up to me and commenting on how attractive I looked.
I look back now and have a good laugh about it. Like a lot of street people he was very quick to pick up on any apparent weaknesses in someone's life. He found one of mine and thoroughly enjoyed what, to him, was just a game. I, however, was not up for playing his game. This said more about me than him.

AN ADVENTURE LIKE NO OTHER | *Warwick Murphy*

The time spent working with this team gave me a passion for these people which is still with me today. I like to believe that much of it came from my upbringing in the Salvation Army. We always had "street people" in our meetings at the Sallies. As a kid, I remember homeless people and alcoholics being in the meetings. They were dirty and smelly, but they were included and involved. If there was a social function on, someone would look for them and include them. It never seemed strange to me that these people were around, it just seemed normal. Today, if I talk to people about who we work with, I am often asked if I ever feel scared or worried. I can honestly say that I don't. I feel very comfortable around them and, mostly, enjoy being with them. But life was about to take another unexpected turn.

The church I was attending, like a lot of similar fellowships back then, did not have a strong understanding of Theology. There was a lot of emotion and zeal but not a lot of depth. Churches like this are prone to get lopsided in their teaching. This church was no different. Within months of my beginning with this church they started to develop a line of teaching which became known as "heavy discipleship." This was a movement that took hold in a number of charismatic fellowships across the world at that time. The outworking in many cases being that people were expected to submit many of the major decisions in their lives to the church leadership to sanction. Eventually, the church I was attending split and many people left the church, having been "excommunicated" by the leadership, and many of those people were hurt deeply. Many others stayed, including my friend, Neil. So here I was six months into being a Christian and already I had been excommunicated! I believed at the time that the leadership of the church was wrong, and I have never changed my view on that for one minute, hence the excommunication was not a painful thing at all. Since that time, I have been privileged to work with some very good leaders. One of the hallmarks of these leaders is their humility and willingness to seek counsel from others.

Chapter 5 Go, or Stay?

One group who left the church gathered around Tony Fitzgerald. Tony had felt that God wanted him to take a team to England to work with a drug rehab center over there called the Red House which was run by a man called Vic Ramsay. Vic was quite a character in his day. He always had something happening. One of his sayings back then was, *"If you can see the end of your vision then your vision is too small."* Some of us who had been excommunicated from the church had been meeting together with Tony and it seemed like a natural progression to me to consider joining this team that Tony was putting together. However, it was not a matter of just joining a team. I needed to know if God was in this or not. This was my first experience of submitting my choices to God. I needed to pray.

As I prayed, I felt God clearly lead me to join this team. By now I was in a relationship with the girl I had met at the Bible school, June. She had caught my eye during my week at the Bible school and I thought to myself, *"I wouldn't mind marrying that chick one day."* For those who know my wife, this next piece will not come as a surprise. June is not a shy person and knowing that I might be heading overseas with a team of people quite soon, she said to me one night, *"If it was a leap year I would ask you to marry me."* I looked at her and said, *"If it was a leap year I would say yes!"* Not the most romantic proposal, but then again, 46 years later we are still together. She truly is an amazing woman who has been by my side in everything we have done.

At this time, June was in the middle of the first year of nursing, having recently completed the training. She really wanted to finish this first year in Melbourne, so, while I left for overseas, she stayed behind and then flew to England to join me later. We got engaged just before I left and were apart for seven months and then got married six weeks after she arrived in England. Not the ideal way to do an engagement, and I certainly would not encourage it as a pattern for an engagement, but it worked for us.

The team traveling to the UK consisted of a number of singles, like myself, and four families with a total of eight children. These people had left homes and businesses to follow what they perceived as the leading of God in their lives.

Chapter 6
A Different World

I had moved to Melbourne in August of 1974 and here I was, six months later, in March, 1975, flying to the other side of the world. I never did finish my planned travel around Australia. I was detoured to the UK. God had a bigger vision for my life than I could ever imagine.

We arrived at Heathrow airport early in the evening. We then had a long drive up to the town of Newark, in the midlands, not far from Nottingham. We were hosted by good people from the Newark Salvation Army. Our team leader had been in Britain earlier in the year and spent some time with the local Salvation Army Officers in the town, Bill and Jean Davidson. Bill was very well-known in the Salvation Army as he had been a member of a band called the Joystrings. Bill is a very gifted musician and songwriter. Bill and Jean have since gone on to plant a church in upstate New York, USA, and have also been involved with ministries in South America and Liberia. The people from the Salvation Army in Newark housed us and welcomed us into their lives. God had been doing a great work in their lives over the preceding months. I was billeted with a young couple from the church who were both teachers.

It was here in Newark that I had my first introduction to culture shock. I had not been expecting any culture shock. I had expected, due to the close history of Australia and Britain, that things would be the same. I was wrong. This young couple had two cars. Robin Reliants. These cars only had three wheels. I had only ever seen pictures of such things before. Every time I was in one of these cars, I expected it to fall over. There were many other things that I found different to "home," but, suffice to say, I quickly became aware that this step to the other side of the world was going to be more different than I had imagined.

The house this couple owned was much smaller than what I was used to. There was no laundry. The washing machine was in the kitchen. The walls in the house were lined with polystyrene under the wallpaper as a form of insulation. The back garden was small and totally under cultivation with vegetables. As I walked past building sites, I noticed that most of the workers were wearing collars and ties, with the inevitable flat cap. Due to the time of year, it was cold and wet. People queued at the fish and chip shop instead of just barging in as we did in Australia. I could go on. So many things were different, and this difference was actually exciting to this naïve young man from Australia. This was so different to what I had expected. And isn't that just what it is like as we walk the road that God has for us? We think we know what is ahead when in fact God has a much bigger plan than we can even imagine. I guess this is where we begin to learn to trust Him every step of the way. I guess, if we knew the extent and detail of what God had in store, would we have taken that first step? I think not.

So here we were. A team of people from Australia, sitting in a small town in the middle of England, wondering what on earth we should be doing. We had come to this part of Britain to get involved at the Red House, but, although we had a good relationship with that place, it never developed into anything of substance. So, rather than just sit down and wait for an angelic visitation, which I believe can be quite rare, we decided we needed to be active. A couple of the team leaders had been to London and seen things that they thought we could get involved with.

Chapter 6 A Different World

So, each Friday night a group of us would make the 150-mile journey down to London to reach out to the many young people gathered around Piccadilly Circus. For our friends in Newark this was a very strange thing to be doing. Back then people in Britain did not travel great distances. They tended to stay close to home. We met several people in Newark who in fact had never been to London. They stayed in Newark, apart from the annual holiday in a Bed and Breakfast hotel in Skegness.

This was an exciting time for me. A young, naïve, Aussie boy in one of the biggest cities in the world. A city that seemed to be the center of the world. London was buzzing. This was a time when so many of the "norms" of life were being challenged. The Beatles, the Rolling Stones, and the Who were impacting the world with their music. Carnaby St and The Kings Rd were where all the latest and weirdest fashions were to be seen. This was also the beginning point for the many young people, who were aiming to travel to places like Kabul and India, down what was called the "Hippy trail" to find enlightenment with some guru in the east. You could even get a ride on what was called "the Magic Bus" all the way to Asia. London and Amsterdam were the jumping off places for these young people.

Long hair, wild clothes, drugs, and free sex were the mantras of the day. "If it feels good, do it" was the statement on everyone's lips. While this has become known as "the '60s", in fact, a lot of it happened in the '70s. It truly was a different time. People's recollections of what it was paint a very limited view of this period. Many people think it was simply about "sex, drugs, and rock and roll." Statements like the one attributed to John Lennon, when he said, ***"If you can remember the '60s then you weren't there,"*** have not helped. Many of the hippies were actually very intelligent people. Although emotions through this time drove a lot of what was happening, this was also a time when very serious questions were being asked about the society that we lived in. Questions about politics, financial systems, nuclear proliferation, and the inequality in society that drove a wedge between rich and poor.

In many ways, the motives were good, but the dreams being peddled by the prophets of the time were lost in a haze of drugs. People such as Timothy Leary and Andy Warhol were telling us to just "drop out and turn on". You cannot bring lasting change to a society from a foundation of emotion and drug-induced haze. The so-called "summer of love" in San Francisco lasted for a few months and ended in broken relationships and hurting people.

This period was indeed a pivotal time in the history of the Western World. In the immediate period after the Second World War societies were focused on rebuilding, but the inequities that were inherent in the systems they were building needed challenging. The confrontation between the capitalist systems of the world and the communist systems was frightening. The nuclear arsenals were constantly being built up and many people believed we were on the edge of destruction. The build-up of these nuclear arsenals led many to believe that governments were committed to a policy of Mutual Assured Destruction, or MAD for short.

In South Africa, the cries of the people living under the repression and prejudice of a system of apartheid were being heard across the world. Demonstrations were a regular thing outside South African embassies across the world.

In many ways the Christian church was seen to be aligned with many of these systems and therefore found themselves in turmoil as well. Rather than seek to look at this with eyes of understanding, sadly what we saw was a reaction, rather than a considered response. When John Lennon stated at one point that the Beatles were more popular than Jesus, large parts of the church went ballistic and hardened their conservative attitudes. Musicals, such as "Hair", which included large amounts of nudity, and Godspell, were called out as blasphemous by church leaders.

There seemed to be upheaval everywhere. In the USA and Australia, there were demonstrations against the Vietnam War. In

Chapter 6 A Different World

the UK, there was a growing "peace" movement focused on how the British government was dealing with the Cold War against Soviet Russia. Yet God was still working in this period. Many important organizations were birthed during this time. Campus Crusade for Christ was reaching out to the universities in the US with a reasoned message about Jesus. Youth With a Mission was born during this time. They were mobilizing and training young people to take the message of Jesus across the world. Dilaram Ministries were focused on reaching out to the hippies on the trail to Asia. They set up houses down that trail to meet and interact with the travelers. The L'abri Fellowship, led by Francis Schaeffer, one of the most brilliant thinkers of that time, was operating in Switzerland and answering the questions that these young people were asking. Interestingly, these groups were seen as "Para Church" organizations. They were not seen as part of the overall church, even though, in fact, they were, and are. I wonder if these so-called Para Church organizations would not be needed if the Church were actually doing what it should in its own neighbourhood? When we look at history, we can see that God moves in times when we think He is silent. He has always had a remnant of people carrying the Torch of the Testimony through these times.

In the center of Piccadilly Circus in London stood the Shaftesbury Memorial Fountain. This statue is often incorrectly called Eros as it is, in fact, an image of Anteros, the brother of Eros. The statue was designed to commemorate the philanthropic work of Lord Shaftesbury. Piccadilly Circus is a large roundabout for traffic and this statue was situated right in the middle. Nowadays, the traffic has been redirected around the statue. However, at this time, on the steps around the statue were young people from all over the western world, sitting, talking, and deciding what was the next thing to be involved with. Directly under Piccadilly Circus was the Piccadilly Tube station. This is a circular set up leading to various underground train lines. It was here in the station that every Friday night we found dozens of young people doped out on various drugs. They knew what time the dealers would arrive, and you could almost set your watch by it.

They would purchase their drugs and head into the public toilets to prepare their "hit" and then inject before leaving the station. Some of these people were what you would call "weekend warriors" just in town for a good weekend after which they would head back to the parents house and their regular job. Most however were runaways looking for excitement.

London has always been a place where people believe they will find something special. I call it "the Dick Whittington syndrome." The story goes that Dick Whittington (c. 1354 – 1423) was a young man who came to London to find his fortune. He ended up becoming the Lord Mayor of London. Sadly, for the people we met, there was to be no call to be the mayor. Each one of them had a sad, tragic story. They looked terrible as the continued use of drugs drained the life out of them. Someone said to me once that drug use is death on time payment. Such a true statement, and we were watching people dying in front of us. I recall one evening we had just descended the steps into the ticket area when I saw a young girl, maybe 17 years old, just a few years younger than me. She had just come from the public toilets where she had injected her latest purchase of heroin. When I saw her, she was literally sliding down the wall in a drug induced stupor. We didn't know if this was an overdose or not, so we called an ambulance. They were with us fairly quickly. The ambulance guys surveyed the scene and then one of them looked at us and said, *"So what do you want us to do?"* The callousness in his voice was surprising. We said, *"She needs to be taken to a hospital."* He responded, saying, *"We see this every day. We will take her to the hospital, they will dose her up with vitamin C and she will be back here within the hour."* He said, *"I appreciate your concern, but you won't save anyone here."* I think we were all quite stunned. So, they took her away in the ambulance and within two hours she was back in the station looking for another hit. Those scenes have never left me. I was impacted deeply by what we had just seen. I knew that I had been only a choice away from being in a similar situation only a few months before this. Truly, "there but for the grace of God, go I". The empty look

Chapter 6 A Different World

on the faces of these young people I can still see. They were people that God created and loved. People who should have had so much to look forward to and yet they were being cheated by life, and the community was being cheated out of whatever gifts and abilities they could have contributed. There are seminal moments in our lives that make an impact on us. For me this was such a time. Moments like this confront us with questions, "How am I going to live my life from now on?" "What is my response to what I have just seen?" "Can I go back to live the Australian dream and settle down on my quarter-acre block with a triple fronted brick veneer house, three and a half children, TV in every room? Or will I respond differently and allow myself to become someone who might be able to bring some change to these broken lives? To lay down my own dreams for the sake of a lost generation?" Having seen the faces of lost dreams in the hollow eyes of the people we met in London how could I not respond. Even while I write this, I am still moved by the memories of those times in the Piccadilly Tube station.

Chapter 7

Youth With a Mission

During our time in Newark, Vic Ramsay held a conference in a big tent on the grounds of the Red House. He had invited speakers from around the world to the conference. One such speaker was Don Stephens. Don was one of the leaders of a group called Youth With a Mission (YWAM). I had heard a bit about this organization, but this was my first introduction to it in a serious way. Our team leader, Tony, had a number of conversations with Don about why we were in England and out of those conversations came the next step in my adventure, and involvement with the organization that was to become a large part of our lives from then on.

After his conversation with Don Stephens, and after praying, Tony felt that this was where God was leading us as a team. Then the team prayed about this and we felt that this was our next step. So, over the next days, we made the move from Newark, in the midlands, to Ifield hall in Sussex. We didn't all move at the same time and, in fact, some on the team did not join us in Sussex, although there was no division in relationship. Our friends in Newark were excited for us and we kept in touch with many of them for many years afterwards. In fact, the officers at the Newark Corps eventually resigned their commission as officers and joined us at Ifield Hall as they felt God lead them to a new field of ministry.

The move to YWAM

Three months after arriving in the UK we joined Youth With a Mission (YWAM) at their base at Ifield Hall in Crawley, Sussex. Ifield Hall was a large facility not unlike an English Manor House. It had extensive grounds and housed upwards of 70 people at times. It served as a training base for YWAM UK. People would come for a three-month lecture phase in a school of evangelism. After the school, they went off in a bus on a three-month field trip to either the Middle East and Africa, or behind the Iron Curtain. The Middle East field trip took them to many of the places we read about in the Bible and the other trip gave the students an opportunity to learn what it was like to live in a part of the world where persecution was the norm for Christians. After the field trip, they returned to England for the third phase of their program, a summer of service. This involved small teams being attached to a local church and participating in reaching out to the community around the church with the message of hope. This was where the students were able to put into practice what they had learned in the lectures. Apart from the School of Evangelism students there were other staff living at Ifield Hall. YWAM had a pizza shop running in the nearby town of Crawley and the team that ran that lived at Ifield Hall. There was a small team running a printing shop producing pamphlets and newsletters. There were staff running the kitchen and the garage as well as a thriving vegetable garden out the back. There was always something happening and things to be involved in.

The team of Australians ventured into this new situation. This period was like Boot Camp for me! Every day there was something new to learn. YWAM, even at that stage, had extensive ministry around the world and there was a constant stream of people dropping in on their way to somewhere else. The teaching in YWAM in those days was life changing. I had heard the Gospel all my life but now I was hearing about the fear of the Lord, the reality and practice of forgiveness, restitution, hearing the voice of God, the character of God. I could go on! People like Loren Cunningham, Floyd McClung, Corrie Ten Boom, Joy Dawson, Brother Andrew, Winkie Pratney, and Gordon Olsen–these people were not just teachers, they were involved in day-to-day ministry all over the world. Floyd McClung had started a ministry called Dilaram, which had established houses along what was called the "Hippy Trail" from Amsterdam to Delhi to minister to the thousands of young people who were making that pilgrimage looking for enlightenment. Corrie Ten Boom had lived through a concentration camp during the Second World War, seeing her sister die in that place. She wrote a book called *The Hiding Place* and had spent her time since the war speaking on the issues of forgiveness. Brother Andrew was involved in smuggling Bibles into countries behind the Iron Curtain at a time when authorities in those countries were arresting and imprisoning people simply for having a Bible. All of them opened my mind to things I had never understood, but one of them, Harry Conn, was the one who actually made me think, not just listen. This man was in fact, an engineer, who spent much of his time teaching the Bible. He was not interested in people just listening to him. He really made us think about, and question, the propositions he put forward. I have since realised that too often we can say that we believe something without really understanding the depth of a particular subject. It is important to actually learn to think and to realize why we might believe what we say we believe. Ravi Zacharias put it this way. He said he saw his role as, **"Helping thinkers to believe, and believers to think."** In all honesty I was learning to "think".

We were pushed to consider just how these subjects that I have listed above, if taken seriously, will change our value systems and our very lives. I believe that when Jesus' disciples actually started to realize just what Jesus had been teaching them they then went

Chapter 7 Youth With a Mission

out and turned the world upside down. It is these subjects that drive people to leave the things they have known, and embark on a whole different lifestyle because they now have a new understanding of who God is and His purposes. They have a new understanding of the value that God places on a human life. They have a new understanding of the difference between the culture they had grown up with and the culture of the Kingdom of God that Jesus taught. I will forever be grateful for those times and that input. It has served me well over the years. As Joy Dawson used to say, we have been *"spoiled for the ordinary"*.

A lot of this teaching was based around the character of God and the government of God. I firmly believe that if we do not have a good understanding of God's character then we will struggle to understand many of the things that happen to us, and around us. When things don't go the way that we thought they should, where do we turn? When we don't get the answer to prayer that we had expected, how do we believe that any prayer will be answered? When we read about people being persecuted for their faith, how do we reconcile that with a God of Love? So many questions that we all have at times are easier to handle when we truly know that God is indeed faithful, long suffering, patient, kind, just, merciful, and loving. We often talk about the truth of the Bible, but the truth of the Bible only holds true if God is true to His character that we read about in the Bible. The veracity of this book is based wholly on God's character. If we are not constantly growing in our knowledge of and belief in His character then how do we develop the relationship with God that we often tell people is so important, and one of the things that makes Christianity different to any other faith?

Understanding the government of God helps us get a bigger picture for the future. I do not need to see a long way down the road. I can trust that God sees it all and wherever I am, if I am in relationship with Him, I can be at peace.

The narrative we hear from so many in the world today is that God is a killjoy and is only out to spoil and limit our enjoyment. It seems to me that many of the people who promote these images of God have never seriously read the scriptures at all and made no study of faith, but they still feel they can speak authoritatively on the subject of faith in a God who they have never taken the time to learn about. The scriptures actually paint a very different picture indeed. The book of Psalms is full of wonderful images of the character of God, telling us how faithful He is toward us. They note His joy over His people, and His willingness to assist us and come alongside us in times of difficulty. A serious reading of the Bible shows us a God who governs from love. A God who wants to hold mankind very close to His heart. A God who has blessed us with free will, even when He knew that this aspect of our creation had within it the ability to break His own heart. Like any good father He seeks only our best and highest good. To do that, like any good father, it means that He places boundaries around our behavior. He teaches us that there are consequences, both good and bad, for our choices. It is often these areas that people use to paint a picture of a mean-hearted God. But isn't this what any parent does? Do we not place boundaries around our children, for their safety and benefit? Do we not teach them that there are consequences for their choices? And though at times our children may think we are mean, do they not come to us later in life and thank us for our good parenting? The truth is that God is good and as we learn to know Him, we are drawn towards Him and want to live a life in line with His will.

There is so much more to these subjects, of course, but the teaching we had all those years ago has helped us to continue on this road. Have there been doubts? You bet! Have there been days where we seemingly had no idea what was going on? You bet! But God has continually proven Himself faithful through it all. Today I am confident that the direction He leads us in is the right one.

One activity that took place everyday on a YWAM base was a time of intercession. We were all in different prayer groups and each morning each group would meet to wait on God to see what we should pray about that day. This, again, was a whole new world to me. To let God direct our prayers. This was not a time of haphazard praying. It was a group of people praying for the same situation for a concerted period of time. Then the groups would meet together and share what they had been praying about. It was amazing to this naïve young Australian how many times we found several groups praying for the same situation. Intercession is one of the foundation stones of YWAM

Learning to discern what some have called "the voice of God," and others call "the leading of God," has been something that has never left me. Everything that June and I have done since that time has been because we felt directed by God in some way. Did we hear an audible voice at these times? No. But in our quiet times we may have felt led to a particular scripture verse, or have a growing sense that God was opening up something new to us. A new path to walk down. Whenever we have felt God opening up something new we have always taken it to a spiritual leader to hear from their wisdom. We have seen God lead us via a variety of ways over the years. God does speak to His people. The Bible says, **"My sheep hear my voice."** If you are not hearing God speak to you, are you in a position to hear? He is not silent. Someone once said that if God seems far away guess who moved? So true.

Chapter 8

Lessons in Faith

The directors of the YWAM base were a strapping American guy, Lynn Green, and his wife Marti. Lynn had been praying for God to raise up a mobile outreach team to travel to different parts of the UK. This team from Australia fit ideally into what he was wanting. At Ifield Hall our team was joined by a few others and new adventures began. Most of these were adventures of faith. It was at Ifield Hall that I learned my first lesson in trusting God financially. I had listened as various people had testified how God had provided for them either financially or in other ways. So, the day came that I decided I needed to reach out to God with my needs. One of my greatest needs at that time was a new pair of shoes. The ones I had been wearing for some time had a hole in them and I needed new ones. I had seen a pair in a local shoe shop in Crawley that I liked, and they were priced at five pounds. So, I set about praying for God to provide me with five pounds for these shoes. Days went by and nothing happened. More time and by now I was getting angry with God. How come others could testify to His provision but I could not. After all it wasn't going to break His bank. Five pounds against the cattle on a thousand hills, so the Bible says. One day as I was praying, I felt the Lord say, *"What is in your pocket?"* I said I had my last five pounds in my pocket. If I used that to buy the shoes, I would have nothing, so I hung on to my five pounds and still cried out to God to provide. More days went by and the five pounds in my pocket was a constant thought. Eventually I caved in, went out

Chapter 8 Lessons in Faith

and spent my last five pounds and had my new shoes. The lesson being, when we have a need, to use what we have first and then we will see God provide. Firstly, put your hand in your own pocket. After all, whatever is in there is supposed to be His anyway. We are just stewards. Of course, this is one of the lessons from the story where Jesus fed the multitude with five loaves and two fish. He used what they had and saw God do the rest.

This story I have seen repeated many times since. The old hymn says that *"when we have reached the end of our hoarded resources, the Father's full giving has only begun."* It is so true. God was teaching me a valuable lesson that I have never forgotten. And now all these years later we have seen God's provision in so many ways and we are still alive to tell the story.

During these first months in the UK, June and I were living in two different countries. I was there in the UK and June was in Australia. We were writing letters (remember them?) to each other and preparing for our wedding. We were 12,000 miles apart, so that made things a bit difficult. June finally finished her year of nursing in Melbourne and arrived in the UK and we set about serious preparation for our wedding. We wanted Tony Fitzgerald to marry us, but he was not registered in the UK as a marriage celebrant. We had to arrange to get married in the local registry office in Crawley. So, we ended up getting married twice. In the morning at the registry office and in the afternoon in a local Anglican Church with Tony officiating. It was the end of November and cold, but it was a great day. Anyone who was living at Ifield Hall was there and many of our friends from Newark had traveled down to join in the celebrations. The reception was at Ifield Hall and had to be one of the most entertaining receptions I have ever attended. The members of our mobile team had taken it upon themselves to arrange the entertainment for the reception. A very funny evening all round, then we drove off in a Volkswagen Kombi van for a three-week honeymoon traveling around Europe. That is another story all on its own.

AN ADVENTURE LIKE NO OTHER | *Warwick Murphy*

We began our married life living with lots of other people. Our engagement was different than most, being six months apart is not what I would suggest for an engagement and our first years were also going to be different, living in a house with so many other people. However, we enjoyed our time at Ifield Hall and are still in contact with many of the people from that time.

Our team had been tasked with the role of traveling all over Britain with a presentation called *the Last Commandment*. Our aim was to recruit people to travel to Montreal, Canada later in the year for a huge outreach at the 1976 Olympic Games. We had a big bus that we traveled on and every day was a new town and a new church to set up in. On this team, God opened doors that amazed us. I found myself speaking in churches and preaching on the streets of Britain. I led a YWAM team to the Olympic outreach in Montreal. Life was one adventure after another. Whoever said that being a Christian was boring must have been in a different church than me, or, more likely, they had never been a Christian to really find out.

One particular event stands out to me. Our team was at one time traveling to different parts of Britain promoting the coming outreach to be held at the Olympic Games in Montreal in 1976. One part of that tour saw us in Ireland. At this time, Ireland was in the grip of what they called "the troubles". The Irish Republican Army (IRA) was fighting a violent war against the British. They wanted a united Ireland and it seemed that any method to advance their cause was OK. Violence in all its forms was everywhere. People being killed or "kneecapped". Bombs going off. British troops everywhere. Our trip began in Belfast. We had never seen anything like it. Armed troops were on every corner in the city. People had to undergo being frisked just to get to the shops. We were all billeted out to different church families while we were in Belfast for those days. We gave presentations in a number of churches and were treated so well by these people. Then we traveled to Dublin. Before we left that morning for the drive to Dublin, Loren Cunningham, the international leader of YWAM, who was traveling with us for a few days, had

Chapter 8 Lessons in Faith

shared a scripture with us from Psalm 91. It is a Psalm about God's protection. In one part it says, *"You will not fear the terror of night, nor the arrow that flies by day, nor the pestilence that stalks in the darkness, nor the plague that destroys at midday."* As we approached the border between Northern Ireland and the Republic of Ireland, we were confronted with another sight I had never seen. The border post was surrounded by a huge metal fence and barbed wire. The only way in or out of this British military base was by helicopter or armed vehicle. The very scene informed us of just how serious the security situation was. The border is, in fact, in a part of the country that the Brits called "bandit country" due to the heavy presence of the IRA. As we pulled away from the border one of the team reminded us that it was midday as we came through the border and Psalm 91 says that we will be protected at noontime. That was comforting to know, but we were all shocked to hear that the very next day a bus had been pulled over close to the border by the IRA and the driver was hauled out of the bus and executed. Thank you, Lord, for protection.

In early1976, our team were invited to spend three months working with a church in a little town in the south west corner of Wales. A place called Milford Haven. By now our outreach team had become quite international. Team members came from England, South Africa, Zimbabwe, and Australia. We arrived in Milford Haven in two red minibuses and it was not long before we were involved in activity. Although we had been invited to stay for three months, it was not long before we were asked to extend our stay. In the end we were there for 15 months and saw God do amazing things. There was a strong move of God among the young people in the town. The teaching we had heard at Ifield Hall was quickly bearing fruit. We had opened a coffee shop in the town, and we were getting invitations to speak in many of the chapels in the area. It was here that I was given my first opportunity to preach on a regular basis. A little chapel in a neighboring town called Neyland had invited the team to run their services for a time as they had no permanent pastor. Tony, the team leader, asked me to lead the team at these services and preach. I had been reading John Wesley's sermons at the time and figured if it was good enough for John Wesley then it was good enough for me. So, I preached to this little group of people using one of Wesley's sermons, "The almost Christian and the Altogether Christian," as my subject. What I had forgotten was that John Wesley preached under the anointing of the Holy Spirit. I was preaching from my own pride. The results were vastly different. I am sure that at some point I should return there to apologize to all those people who I berated as I tried to emulate John Wesley. After hearing me for three weeks the people in the church asked if our team could please send someone else next week. Embarrassing, but true. Arrogance raised its head in many ways.

However, it was also in this little town that God began to open the door to what has become the rest of our lives. Milford Haven had an unemployment figure of over 20%. Work was difficult to find even if you had a profession. If you were just leaving school and university was not an option, then there was no work. Before long my wife and I found ourselves entertaining a group of around 15 young lads from the town. At heart they were good people but like many young people with nothing else to do they found themselves in bother with the law and were seen by many as the problem kids of Milford Haven. I ended up going to court with one of the group leaders who had been caught stealing cigarettes from a local store. The fact that someone was prepared to speak in court on behalf of her son was a great mystery to this young man's mother. No one had ever shown any concern for him before. Most evenings these young men would arrive at our house and we would end up playing some board game or other with them. If they had been fishing through the day, they would drop by to show off their catch. They quickly became a very important part of our lives and I believe that we had become an important part of their lives too.

Looking back, it was here that we began to see there was something different about these kids. We would invite them to one of the outreach events that we ran, or church on Sundays, and they would always turn us down. For them, church was for respectable people and they did not see themselves in that light. It was at this point that we started to see that they were still important even if they never came to church. We continued to enjoy their company and made sure that they understood that attendance at church, or making a commitment as a Christian, was not a prerequisite for our friendship. They, like all of us, had inherent value simply because God had created them in His image.

Francis Shaeffer says in his book, *Escape From Reason,* **"We cannot deal with people like human beings, we cannot deal with them on the high level of humanity, unless we really know their origin— who they are. God tells man who he is. God tells us that He created man in His image. So, man is something wonderful. The Bible says that you are wonderful because you are made in the image of God, but that you are flawed because at a space-time point of history, man fell."**

It was not an option for us to reject them, but it was indeed our privilege to continue to be open to them and let them know that they were valued anyway. The beauty of the Gospel is that "Christ died for us while we were yet sinners." He did not, and does not, wait for us to reform ourselves before He accepts us. As the power of this became real, I began for the first time to wonder why people ever reject God. He is so awesome.

Milford Haven was many things to us. It was the place where God taught us many things. It was where He began to develop our understanding of what He wanted us to do for the rest of our lives. It was like a doorway for us. It seemed as though God held the door open just wide enough for us to see something of the future without ever revealing the whole picture. We were also shown things about ourselves and discovered abilities that He had placed there but they had remained unseen to us. Through good leadership, and the commitment of the other team members we were going through spiritual adolescence and making discoveries that would change our lives.

As I said earlier, we had been invited to Milford Haven for a few months, but this turned into 15 months. We were doing open-air outreach on the main street of the town. We had opened up a small "coffee shop" in the town, and as time went on we eventually rented a shop front where we held meetings and ran teaching sessions. It was here in this little town in Wales that we saw God move amongst the young people from the local church. The message we were sharing was one of the Lordship of Jesus. If He is not Lord of all then He is not Lord at all in your life. This was a new message that they had not heard. We watched as God began to move amongst the elders in this little church. There was an excitement as to what God was doing.

The church where we were based was a little chapel called Rehoboth. It proudly stated that it was a Welsh Presbyterian and Calvinistic Methodist church. I am still not sure if that is an oxymoron. The minister of the church had been there for 25 years. In the middle of this move of God this minister stood up in his church one Sunday and testified that, after all his years of preaching and leading a church, he had finally surrendered his life to Christ. Wow. What a testimony.

2nd Faith Lesson.

Milford Haven is one of Britain's deepest seaports. It is located on the South West tip of Wales in the county of Dyfed. A truly picturesque place with lovely beaches and coastlands. The team had rented a shop front plus the upstairs space at one end of the main street. This was where we held team meetings and open meetings with the youth in the town. June and I lived in the manse of one of the town chapels on the other side of town. It meant a decent walk through the town, across the harbor inlet and up a hill on the other side before cresting the hill and finding our place down the other side.

Chapter 8 Lessons in Faith

Milford Haven at times had a fog that would drift in and make visibility at night-time quite difficult. It was on one of these nights, after we had finished a meeting at the shop front, I was making my way back home through a very heavy fog. At the time we had no money, and I mean "no money". Those times, even though we are praying and seeking God, are still times when we question what we are doing. Should we just go back to Australia? Does God really provide for His people as we think He does, etc., etc.?

While walking home that night I was pondering all this. I was cold, I was hungry, I was a little depressed. I felt like I was not being the provider for my wife that I should be. So, I walked along, having a very one-sided conversation with the Lord about all this. After I crossed the little bridge over the waterway, I began the climb up the hill. Halfway up this hill was a Fish and Chip shop, and I could vaguely make out the shop sign through the fog as I made my way up the hill. The smell from the shop drifted down the hill through the fog and into my nose. On a cold damp night the smell for someone who was feeling a little low was no doubt magnified. Fish and Chips just have that heart-warming appeal to an empty stomach like little else.

I remember saying to the Lord, in a rather strong tone, *"Is it really too much to ask for some hot chips on a cold night?"* Almost instantly, I felt the Lord say to me, *"Heaven is worth a lot more than hot chips."* It was a small rebuke, but also a challenge to me. What was God saying? I believe He was saying that life as a Christian is full of challenges, and disciples need to learn how to stand in the tough times. In the book of Jeremiah, in chapter 12, God says, *"If you can't run with footmen and they have tired you out, then how can you compete with horses?"* God had us in a training school of discipleship, and He uses any circumstance to teach us. God does not waste anything. He sees a much bigger picture than we do. The lessons we learn from Him are not necessarily about what is happening today. They are, more than likely, learning for the future. Just like with a football coach or with learning a trade, we are being taught to look further down the road. I was still learning that lesson.

I have never forgotten that little conversation. It has held me in good stead many times when funds have been short. Father God has much to teach us as His followers and He uses our everyday lives to bring home to us the pearls of His wisdom.

1976.
Montreal Outreach to the Olympic Games.

In the summer of 1976, I was part of a team from YWAM UK that headed to the Olympic Games that were being held in Montreal. YWAM had run a big outreach at the previous games in Munich. At those games in Munich, a number of Israeli athletes were murdered by terrorists. The shock waves went round the world. In the aftermath of the terrorist attack the YWAM teams had led a time of public prayer which was attended by many people who had simply come to the games to see the best, sports people in the world perform and were now in shock at what had occurred. Those who attended included Olympic athletes, police, and city officials. It truly was a time when people realized how short life can be and were looking for some way of dealing with the shock, grief, and pain of what had occurred just days earlier.

Now four years later, YWAM was leading another outreach in Montreal. Literally thousands of people had come for this outreach. We were all camped outside of Montreal and would be bussed into the games area each day. Here was another time of learning on the run. The way the games area was set up was such that the athletes had to walk through a large public area to get from the village to the stadium. We had the opportunity to speak with athletes from all over the world. Remember it was a time when the Soviet Union was basically closed to Christian witness. Many people became Christians during that time, and I had learned new things about myself and about God.

Chapter 8 Lessons in Faith

At the beginning of the outreach, we were all separated into different large teams. These large teams were then broken down into smaller teams of six to ten people. I was asked to lead a cluster of three of these small teams. I figured that someone had got something wrong as I certainly did not see myself as a leader of any sort. However, my arrogance was still quite large in my life and I took the role on, despite my large self-doubt. Apparently, the leader of the larger team had been given my name as someone who could lead the smaller group, so I found out later. It seemed that someone was seeing something in me that I could not see at all. This was to be the first of several similar occasions where this happened. As we walk the road that God leads us down, we discover that He knows what is inside us far more than we do. He knows what gifts and abilities He has implanted in us. The reason that we do not see these things is that the world we grow up in usually tells us something different about ourselves. I was thankful for those people on my small teams. They were very encouraging and supportive, even though I am sure that they could sense my immaturity and lack of confidence in the role.

As everyone in YWAM is responsible for raising their own support, getting to Montreal was a big challenge. June and I had some funds in the bank that paid for my return airfare, and that was about it. I recall sitting in Montreal airport waiting for our flight back to the UK with the rest of the team. We managed to scrape together enough money for one cup of coffee between us all, and that was it.

Chapter 9

Miracles and Prayer

Towards the end of 1977 June was pregnant and we believed it was the right time to return to Australia. We had been away for three years and felt that we should get back to see family. We thought it would only be a relatively short time in Australia, but we were wrong. We headed to Canberra when we arrived home as this was where the YWAM base in Australia was located. We arrived home at the same time as Tom and Di Hallas and their family. Tom went on to become the YWAM director for Australia and the Pacific region, but at this time he believed that God wanted to establish a YWAM Discipleship Training School (DTS) in Canberra. Prior to this, however, YWAM had organized an outreach in Canberra to coincide with the Pacific Games that were to be held that year. Thousands of athletes and their trainers and other staff would be in Canberra from right across the Pacific region to compete in these games. Hundreds of people came from around Australia and overseas to participate in this outreach. We were all based in an old hostel-style facility in the suburb of Ainslie. This was where the pre-outreach training took place. Each day a different person taught on issues of communication of the Gospel, etc., to prepare everyone for the outreach. Included in the training, of course, was teaching on intercession and prayer.

The head cook at the facility, John Savage, was a nonbeliever but was always hanging around at the back of the lecture hall listening to the speakers. John was a very big man and had a reputation as

Chapter 9 Miracles and Prayer

a hard man in Canberra. He drove a huge "yank tank" of a car, with a loaded shotgun under his seat, so he informed us. He also controlled a number of prostitutes in Canberra. However, he was also a very open sort of character and got on well with everyone. Mind you, we did not know the dark side of his life at this point. At the end of the outreach, John committed his life to Christ and went on to join up with us later in London. More about that later.

1978. Argentina

After the Pacific Games outreach, the concentration became focused on the DTS. June and I became staff on this first DTS in Australia, during which time our first child, Janna, was born. After this school and before the next one, myself and a friend, Bob Heywood, traveled to various parts of Australia, promoting the next international YWAM outreach to be held in Argentina to coincide with the World Cup soccer tournament in 1978. I went on to lead a team to Argentina where again I found I had lots to learn.

The World Cup Soccer Tournament is one of the largest sporting events in the world. YWAM had already held outreaches at the Munich Olympics and the Montreal Olympics, so it had lots of experience at such events. Thousands of people arrived in Argentina for the outreach. As the football matches were spread through several different cities, so we were also divided up into teams in each of those cities. I ended up in the city of Cordoba where we were based in a large Catholic church facility. Here we were divided up into smaller teams and the basic program was: half of the teams would go into the city each day while the other half stayed back for prayer and teaching. Everybody was paired up with someone else from their team for the duration of the outreach. I was privileged to be teamed up with a guy from Tonga, Isilelie Taukolo, or Issy for short. Issy was a typical large Tongan man. I was glad I never faced him on a football field. I believe that he was in some form of leadership back in Tonga, but that was about all that I knew about him. Each day that our team went into town we usually headed for the main plaza. This was a large park like space with a fountain in the middle and a large statue of San Martin. Jose De San Martin (1778-1850) was widely recognized as the man who led Argentina to freedom from the Spanish. He was the great liberator of this country. To me this sounded like the ideal place to preach. So, I preached in this plaza, at the base of the statue of their liberator, but I spoke about the greatest Liberator of us all, Jesus. At this time, Argentina was mainly a Catholic country and Protestants were a sidelined group of people. Most people, although church-goers, had never heard the Gospel message. In many of their churches the Bible was still in Latin and read by the priest. People were eager to receive the Spanish Bibles that we were handing out and, as we preached in the plaza, hundreds would stop to listen.

One of the people who stopped was a young man in a wheelchair. He was well known by the people in the square as he begged every day in the square. Every day we were there this man would come and listen to the preaching and want to talk with the team. One day Issy said to me, *"I think God wants me to pray for this young man's healing."* This was a whole new ball game for me. I understood preaching and sharing your faith with someone but had never been in a position to see anyone get healed, so as you can imagine I was surprised by this statement. I had read in books that God healed people but reading it in a book and actually expecting someone to be healed are two different things. However, wanting to be seen as a man of faith and power, not a man of paste and flour, I supported what Issy wanted to do. The term hypocrite comes to mind as I write this.

So, the next time we were in the plaza, Issy spent a lot of time with this young man telling him, through an interpreter, that he believed that God wanted to heal him and enable him to walk, but the greater thing God wanted to do was to be a part of his life through salvation. By the time Issy had finished talking to this

Chapter 9 Miracles and Prayer

young man, word had spread through the plaza that Issy was going to pray for his healing. Hundreds of people had gathered. All of them knew this young man and had seen him in the wheelchair for years. Eventually Issy stepped back from the crouching position he had been in while talking to this man. In fact, he took a number of steps backwards and in a loud voice prayed a short prayer for healing and in a commanding voice said, ***"In the name of Jesus get out of that chair and walk."*** The silence in the plaza was amazing. Every eye was on the man in the wheelchair. For a few moments it seemed like nothing was going to happen. And then I saw what I had not believed. This young man struggled to his feet and took a step. And then another step. Each step he took he got stronger. He then proceeded to walk all around the plaza to the shouts and encouragement of the crowd. I, and everyone else, had just seen a miracle. The team spread out through the crowd to talk about Jesus and salvation. Many lives were changed that day, including my own. God had just revealed Himself to me in a new way. He is the same yesterday, today, and forever. He healed when Jesus walked the earth and He still heals today. Do I still have questions about the whole issue of healing? Yes, I do. But I cannot doubt what I witnessed that day.

One of the other things that impacted me on that outreach was to see, I believe for the first time in my life, someone groaning and travailing in prayer for those who did not know Jesus. Again, I had read about it in books and in the Bible but had never seen such a thing.

As I have said the facility where we were housed was a typical old Catholic place with four sides built around an open square with a fountain in the middle. Joy Dawson had been teaching that morning and informed us that she felt we should set up a prayer chain to intercede for the outreach. She said that she and Loren Cunningham would begin the prayer chain. After the teaching session, I had gone outside for a walk. When I returned, I became aware of a noise like someone in pain. I noticed other people looking towards the center of the square. As I followed their line of sight, I could see Loren Cunningham, the founder of YWAM, and Joy Dawson, both sitting on chairs next to the fountain. Joy was groaning like she was in pain. It was not a quiet groan. It was coming from deep inside her. And then I saw something I have never seen before. Joy Dawson, dressed in a lovely dress, her hair coiffed nicely, suddenly fell from the chair to the ground. She was face down on the ground and all I could hear was, **"Lord, give us souls. Give us souls,"** as she pounded the ground with her fist. She was crying for these people in Argentina that they would come to know the source of all life. The prayer life of us all went up a notch after that. We did see people come to know this wonderful Father God of ours. People like Joy Dawson, and so many other teachers we have sat under, are not into what they are doing for financial gain, or public acclaim. They have an understanding of the lostness of so many people and a heart to see these people come to know the source of all life.

Many other things happened during that outreach and I came back to Australia with a different drive in my heart.

Chapter 10

Time Out

After the first DTS in Canberra, we stayed on as students on the second DTS in Australia. Possibly the only YWAMers to be able to say that.

It was after this school that we felt it was time to take a break from YWAM and concentrate on being a family with our new little bundle of joy.

We moved to a little flat on the outskirts of Canberra and I took a job as a Sweet chef at the Federal Parliament House. This was a great time to start to understand what a family really is. There is nothing like having that first baby. I recall prior to going to the hospital for the birth that my friend, Tom, said to me, *"You will not believe how you will feel after this baby is born."* How right he was. I recall walking, no floating, out of the hospital that night. There is no way to describe that feeling. That day, everything changed again. We had a new life in our family, and we had to learn what it meant to be parents. Talk about daunting. I always figured that after the child was born a handbook, or manual, should be born with the child because they are all so different and parents could find their role a bit easier, maybe?

One thing having a child does is to move our focus from ourselves to something outside of us. So much of the life this world offers is self-centered. It is about gratifying ourselves. Or as Mark Sayers puts it, it is about radical individualism. Where can I get the biggest emotional high? Can I actually buy enough things to satisfy myself? Am I getting enough job satisfaction? Me, Me, Me. We truly live in a world centered around ourselves and our perceived needs. I have heard it in my counseling room. I have seen it in the dysfunctional families around us. I see it in the influence of so many so-called celebrities on our lives. When a new child arrives, this child should draw our attention away from ourselves towards them. Their needs should become a priority in our lives. However, those needs are not just about feeding and clothing. Those needs are also about us fulfilling, and understanding, our roles as parents. The security of children is not in how much we have in our bank account, or how big our house is. The security children find is in the strength of the relationship of their parents and the boundaries placed around them. I have seen families who have very little, but their children have a sense of security because the parents understand their role.

I worked as the second Sweet chef at the Parliament House in Canberra, the seat of government in Australia. This was the first full kitchen I had ever worked in. My past places of employment had been small cake shops in suburbs of Sydney. This was a big step up. I was totally out of my depth for those first few weeks, however, the head Sweet chef, an extremely talented Austrian guy, was gracious enough to give me space to learn this new environment. As it happened due to my duties there, I was often the last person to leave the kitchen at night. This meant that I was given a ride home in one of the commonwealth cars usually reserved for Members of Parliament. I was able to witness the members of Parliament in close quarters. To prepare and serve meals to parliamentarians, and other dignitaries, such as Prince Charles, who passed through Parliament House. Even though I had a good job which could have developed into a long-term position, I found those two years were a bit of a come down after what we had experienced with YWAM.

Chapter 10 Time Out

Towards the end of this time we both felt we should move from Canberra to Melbourne. So, we packed up the car and headed south. Melbourne is June's hometown and initially we lived with her grandmother. A lovely, gracious woman who welcomed us into her lovely home.

For me, being a 'Sydney sider,' living in Melbourne meant I had to suck up all my prejudices against Victorians. The history of white settlement in Australia is such that Sydney was settled as a convict settlement and that is where those poor souls, who were transported from the UK, first set foot on dry land after possibly 10 months at sea. One of my English friends tells me that only the best people were sent to Australia in those days. They were all handpicked by the best judges in Britain.

Melbourne on the other hand was a free settlement. No convicts here. Since that time, the rivalry between these two cities has never ceased. The rivalry was so bad that when the railway was built between these two cities the track gauge on the NSW side of the border was different to the gauge used on the Victorian side. Which meant of course that passengers had to change trains at the border. I guess politicians were much the same then as now.

People in Sydney figured the best thing to ever come out of Melbourne was the road north. And so it has gone on and will continue no doubt for many years to come.

Now here I was a Sydney boy living in Melbourne.

Melbourne

We joined a church there, found a job, and had no idea what the future held. After the excitement of our time in the UK, life seemed pretty boring. We bought a business and that took up plenty of focus, but we both knew it was not enough. The business we bought was a small shop specializing in Pavlovas and Cheesecakes. It was situated in an upper middle-class area of Melbourne and our products were purchased by people holding parties and celebrations for family or other events in their lives. I was a trained and qualified Pastry Cook, so this business fitted in with those qualifications. However, it did seem a long way from where we had felt God leading us. In fact, I believe we were both confused as to what it was all about. Was the adventure with God over? Was it now back to fitting into Australia and leaving all that we had been through as just another life experience?

I eventually went to see a friend from the church. This was a family that we had grown close to. I think one of the great things we liked about this family was that they always had someone extra staying with them. Not just any visitor but usually a young person who was homeless or had other problems. I shared my frustration with my friend, and he proceeded to tell me about a program the church ran. They called it a halfway house. It was a place for homeless young people, and they were looking for house parents to move in.

We knew this was right and a few months later we moved in to be the house parents for the residents. One of the main concepts of houses, such as this, was that they were supposed to provide what was considered a "normal" home situation for all the young people who came to stay under the roof. I continued to go off to work each day running our business and June stayed at home doing "wifely" things and being mum to these young people. The idea being put forward by the committee that ran the halfway house was that this would create a stable environment for the residents. It would mirror the concept of a home that these kids had never known. What this concept never took into consideration was that the young people who came to stay were often very unstable. They had deep emotional problems such as abandonment, drug use, sexual abuse issues, betrayal, etc. They were not about to be changed simply by living in a "normal" home. These kids needed solid input from people

Chapter 10 Time Out

who understood them. They needed to be confronted at times and taught that their behavior was out of line. They needed to learn that respect went both ways. They needed to be loved like other kids, but recognized as having already been battered by the world and in much deeper needs. Leaving my wife in the house to deal with these situations was not the way to do it. I will never again support that style of housing for needy people.

One of the things that often happens in these places when they are run by churches is that they staff the house with students who attend the church and are looking for cheap accommodation. The thought is that the church youth will be able to relate to the residents because they are young people too. What often occurs instead is that the church youth are confronted by behaviors and lifestyles that they are ill-equipped for, and they have no solid philosophical base to comprehend what is happening, often ending in the church-attending person leaving the house confused and demoralized. In the broader picture, more damage has been done than it was worth. To highlight this point, one of the female residents of the halfway house made herself sexually available to the other three young male residents in the house. Because this liaison occurred outside the house we would never have known until the three young men needed treatment for pubic lice. Then the story came out. The young staff members could not understand how a young girl could do this.

To look at it from a different viewpoint: if, at your church on a Sunday evening, someone came out looking for prayer and they said to the pastor I have a heavy drug problem, I was abused sexually by my father, and I have to be in court on a major charge this week, would the pastor ask one of the young people to pray with this person or look for someone with an understanding of God and who was confident in themselves to come and pray with that person. I am betting that the pastor would look for someone of maturity. Why then do we want to put vulnerable young people, who are still working out who they are and who God is, in such a position?

AN ADVENTURE LIKE NO OTHER | *Warwick Murphy*

I think that too often in our haste to respond to a need we rush in without due planning and consideration. Would we set up a business with inexperienced people or would we look for the person with the credentials to do the job? Even if we saw a business opportunity, we would want to make sure that we had qualified people for the job. We do not ask someone who has no financial understanding to be the church treasurer. Why do we think that dealing with deep hurts in a person's life should be dealt with in a different manner? As you can see, God was already shaping our thinking for the future. He was challenging our beliefs and presuppositions. He knew where He was taking us, but He was also aware that we had some growing to do.

Prior to moving into the house, we were thrilled at the arrival of our second child, a son, Shannon. I don't think anything can prepare us for the fact that no two children are the same. We like to think by the time we are married that we know most of what we need to know about life. Having children is a great way of teaching us just how little we know and how much more we need to know. Shannon was a big boy when he was born, and he is a big man now. He is also totally different to our firstborn. Once again, a handbook would have been helpful. But what a blessing he has been, and still is, to us, and many others.

We struggled through this situation for a number of months before we realized that we could not conform to the wishes of the committee of management, none of whom had any experience of working with damaged lives. This was another problem with this type of arrangement, and we moved to a new house once again and concentrated on our business. Looking back, I can see how we had already become spoiled for the ordinary.

My frustration levels with the daily grind were only highlighted by the growing refugee crisis that was developing in Cambodia at the time. The news reports were full of stories of Pol Pot's murderous regime and the ensuing swarm of refugees who were flooding into refugee camps over the border in Thailand. YWAM was already responding

Chapter 10 Time Out

to this crisis and had taken over the running of a couple of these camps for the UN. I could not believe that I was sitting in Melbourne making Pavlovas while seemingly unable to reach out to help this desperate need. I recall arriving at work each day and crying out to God to make a way where there seemed no way. The situation in Thailand and Cambodia was only serving to impress on me that there was a large percentage of the world in need and here I was making fancy cakes for people in Melbourne. It all seemed so wrong. Although I would have been happy to go to Thailand, I was also aware that I did not have the credentials to do much in that situation, but I knew we needed to be active in working with people in need.

Then it happened. One of those occasions that you never forget, but you know is God. I was sitting in my car at a set of traffic lights on my way home one night when I heard God speak to me. Not an audible voice, but I was so aware that it was Him telling me to prepare to make the return to the UK. I drove home and said to June, **"We are going back to England."** I think I was more excited about getting my hands dirty again rather than understanding what we were going to do. However, God is gracious, and it was not long before it became very clear to us that we were going to London to open up a facility for needy people. Yes, it was that vague, but it was a lot clearer in my mind.

A few months later, we were flying out. By now we had three children, one only 11 months old, Bryn, a second son. By now we were thinking that we had this parenting thing down pat. Except again, where was the handbook? Bryn is different again to the other two children. He is quite black-and-white in how he sees things and has a great sense of humor. It is amazing how your love expands as each child comes along. Learning who this new person is becomes an adventure in itself. Bryn has gone on to bless many, many people and is seeing young troubled lives change due to his involvement and work. Someone could have warned us that they would all be different! We sold everything and raised some support from our church, and we were on our way.

Chapter 11

England again

When we reached England, we discovered that YWAM UK had only recently moved their main operations from the south of England to London. They were based in a facility in Putney, just south of the Thames and in easy reach of the thriving West End district. The director of YWAM, Lyn Green, spent some time with us, bringing us up to speed with the vision of YWAM for London and then he asked what we felt our vision was for returning to London. So, I told him that we wanted to open up a facility for needy people. The vision was as vague as that. Lyn gave us the names of a few contacts that he thought might be able to help and expressed his commitment to us and off he went. This was one of the things I liked about YWAM. They provided a spiritual covering for us, but allowed us to get on with the job. I think Lyn was of the opinion that, if God was really in it, then we would stay and work our way through the tough times, and, if He wasn't really in it, then we would probably head home.

We spent the first few nights at the main facility before moving out to a very large church manse in Fulham, which we shared with another family and a number of singles. We knew it would take time to see something open up for our vision so we joined the mobile outreach team which was operating around London. This team comprised a small group of musicians and a drama team. We would head off each day to a different part of London

Chapter 11 England again

and do some street theater followed by some preaching. There are parts of London that give themselves to what the Salvation Army used to call "Open-Air work". Leicester Sq has several cinemas and restaurants around it. Tourists are wandering around. Buskers as well. Hyde Park Corner is a traditional place in London where people are allowed to step up on a soapbox and talk about anything they like. The history behind this is rather gory. Hyde Park Corner was formally called Tyburn Place. It was where public hangings took place after people had been sentenced to death by a court of law. The tradition was that the condemned person was allowed to speak to the crowd before being executed. Somehow the tradition of being able to speak to a gathering of people had continued so that this was, and still is, a place where you can hear people speaking on a whole variety of subjects.

It was one of the greatest opportunities of my life. It was as a part of this team that God opened another new realm for me. I had done a bit of preaching in churches, and a small experience in Argentina of street preaching, but I had no expectation that this was a field that would fit with me. The difference of preaching in a church and on the streets is quite astounding. In a church, the preacher has usually spent time preparing his sermon. They usually base it round a particular passage of scripture, and they have an amount of time to expound their message. Street preaching is quite different. You have a very short period of time to capture the attention of a passing crowd. If you are talking about something that the passing people are interested in, they may stop to listen. If you are boring, then no one stops, or they just heckle you.

As we were traveling into Leicester Sq one Saturday night, the team leader simply said to me, *"I want you to preach tonight."* I looked at him and said, *"Oh no I don't do that."* His response to me was, *"You will be preaching tonight."* End of subject. He did not give me an option. I could feel panic starting to build up. I had never been, or had any expectation to be, someone with an upfront ministry. Memories of my failed attempts at preaching in Milford

Haven some years back flashed through my mind. What was he thinking asking me to preach on the streets when he had plenty of others to choose from? I walked all round the square trying to work out what to say. The team sang a few songs, the drama team did a couple of skits, and then I was on. I stepped out into the middle of the square and saw a couple hundred people who had been attracted by the drama and music and now it remained to be seen if they would stay to hear a preacher. It was at this point that I found a whole new element in God. I felt a freedom as I spoke like never before. I enjoyed it. I found I could say pretty much whatever I liked and it didn't matter. I enjoyed the hecklers and the ability to interact with them, not simply reject them. When my few minutes had finished I was pleased to see most of the people had stayed and the team was able to move out amongst them and share in a more personal way with individuals that we felt led towards. I have no idea if what I said that night really affected anyone, but God had opened up a door of ministry that I loved, and I found I had a gift for it. This event further opened my eyes to something about how God knows us far better than we know ourselves, similar to what had happened in Montreal. This lesson I have continued to learn, and it has helped me to see things in other people that they cannot see in themselves.

Too often we choose not to attempt things because of our own view of our limitations without realizing that God knows who we really are. I believe that God has placed gifts and abilities in all our lives that we do not know are there until we walk through the door that God guides us to. We are far better off following His lead than trusting our own limited and warped view of ourselves. We have to stop believing the lies in our lives. I am so grateful to that team leader, Alan Beardall, for giving me that opportunity.

So, when I was on the streets, what did I preach about? I tried to be aware of the concerns that the average person had in their lives. At that time in Britain there was a growing anti-apartheid movement along with street demonstrations all aimed at what was happening

Chapter 11 England again

in South Africa at that time. There was the fear about nuclear war, as the Cold War was still on everyone's mind. Someone told me one day that Russia was only 20 minutes away via a Ballistic Missile. Other issues that were relevant in most people's lives were, and still are, to do with relationships, finance, politics, and sexual issues. You will not hear so much on those issues in church, sadly. When we did outreach in Earls Court I always preached about sexual issues as this place was a hotbed of sexual confusion at that time.

Earlier in the book I mentioned a cook in Canberra, John Savage. By now John had made the move to London as well and had joined this team. John had been through a DTS and was keen to work with the street people as he felt they were his people. John was one of the best street preachers I have ever seen. He was a big man physically and he really commanded the footpath where he was preaching. He quickly became a feature and was building relationships with the pimps and sex workers in Earls Court. He was a great guy to have on our team. John loved the Lord dearly, but still had a few things from his old life that were a struggle for him. He had a tough stretch at one point and then managed to get his walk with God back on track. John eventually moved back to Australia where he worked with the Salvation Army just outside of Canberra. John went to be with his Lord a few years back. He was a lovable character with a heart as big as himself.

Chapter 12

Hitting the Streets

From that first night I became a regular preacher with this team as we traveled to Earls Court, Leicester Square, Hyde Park Corner, Notting Hill, and various other parts of London. I was raised in the Salvation Army in Sydney and I felt like we were carrying on that mantle of the early Army as we moved around London. We were confronted with so many different experiences during these times and we could learn something from all of them. The hecklers, who I must admit were very funny at times, were quite amazing in their knowledge of the Bible. There was a man at Earls Court who thrust a live snake into my face one night. There was the ongoing relationship with the police, who were happy for us to do our outreach some nights, but not on others. I well remember Alan being carted off in a paddy wagon because he persisted in preaching after the police had asked him to stop. I also remember the night a lady stood in front of Alan while he was preaching and threatened to hit him with her handbag. Full of fire and faith Alan promptly told her that he was protected by God and that she would not be able to hit him. With which she proceeded to chase Alan around Leicester Square, hitting him with her handbag while he was rebuking her and the devil and claiming God's protection. When Alan finally got back to the team we couldn't stop laughing. Alan was one of the boldest people I have known and his persistence to practice his faith was contagious. The times we had on that team were just another step in God's school of

Chapter 12 Hitting the Streets

practical Christianity, and all helpful for the future. On one of my first preaching times in Leicester Sq, I noticed a gentleman in the front of the crowd who was nodding as I spoke about different issues. He was very encouraging and when I finished speaking, I made my way over to him to see what he may have responded to in my preaching. I introduced myself to him and he smiled broadly and nodded. I then asked if this was his first time in London, and again he smiled broadly and nodded. Then I asked what it was specifically in my preaching that seemed to appeal to him. Once again, he smiled broadly and nodded. By now I was wondering what was going on. Finally, I began to realize something, so I asked if he spoke English. He smiled again and said, "Italiano, Italiano." The man had virtually no English at all. He had just been enjoying the spectacle that our team had put on. I walked away laughing at the situation, and my own pride. While there were many funny events during our time with that team, and there was always something new to learn, there was another side as well.

Each week as we went out into the streets of London we were confronted with the sad, hopeless people. I use the word *hopeless* in the real sense of the word. These were people without hope. The bag ladies, the young people selling themselves in the pinball parlors, the alcoholics and the addicts, the crushed, lonely, and forgotten detritus of a society fighting its way to some unreachable form of perfection. Like any metropolis of over ten million people, there is a group of people who get sifted through the layers and eventually fall through the bottom and are seemingly forgotten. In London on any given night there were, during that time, no less than 20,000 people who slept on the streets. As the shops in the Strand closed, the doorways would be claimed by these people. They would set up their cardboard boxes and dirty blankets in preparation for another night before being moved on in the morning by the shopkeepers. Under the bridges at the Embankment station and in what was known as the Bull Ring they gathered, as well as many other places that they felt would provide them with some form of security and shelter.

Each night as we returned to our house, I was aware of a growing frustration in myself and other team members. We had been able to provide a few hours of friendship to these people, but eventually we had to leave them to the streets. We knew this was not good enough. All this time we were still trying to find a property that we could use to house and minister to some of these needs. As each week passed the frustration grew. The inevitable questions arose. If God has led us here to open a facility, why can't we find it? Did we really hear God? Do we care more than God about these people? These are all good questions to ask but they are also the fodder for prayer and the fertilizer God uses to grow the vision. To put meat on the bones of the vision. In our frustration we need to remember that God is there somewhere. The faith aspect is that we continue to move forward believing that He knows more than us, and that He knows what He is doing.

As we continued to move around London, it became clear to some of the team that we could be far more effective if there was a more permanent presence, as opposed to the constant moving.

One of the results of this was that several team members felt led to set up a YWAM team in Earls Court. The whole team decided that it was important for us to support this move. We made Earls Court a target for our work. We would travel up there four nights a week. Two of those nights we did nothing else but walk around in pairs praying for the area, the other nights we did outreach and spent time getting to know the locals. Earls Court at that time had so many things going on. It was the homosexual center of London, with gay pubs and clubs. There was a large presence of backpackers living in the cheap accommodations around the area and it has long been recognized as the home of Australians living in London, resulting in a couple of Australian pubs and travel agents. There was a large overseas student population there also, and many of these people come from developing nations trying to earn a piece of paper that would open doors in their home country simply because the certificate, or degree, was from a college in London.

Chapter 12 Hitting the Streets

The number of nationalities was amazing. Alongside all of this was a thriving prostitution business with numerous girls working the streets and advertising their wares. Phone booths were plastered with the business cards from these girls. Drug dealers were everywhere, and they had a ready market in many of the groups I have mentioned. If ever there were a place for the church to be seen, this was it. The Earls Court team established an office in the basement of St Jude's Anglican Church. What an appropriate name for a church. St Jude is the patron saint of lost causes and Earls Court was teeming with what the world considered lost causes. So, a team was established, and hard work began. During the day, we were helping people find accommodation, or going to court with them, helping them access health services, or just having a coffee with them. By night, we ran outreach on the main road through Earls Court. We set up outside the station, had a time of worship, some of the team did some drama and then someone would preach. The passing parade quickly taught us that our message had to be relevant to them. The usual Christian clichés were no good here. Whilst the message still needed to be about redemption and salvation, we needed to find a new vocabulary if we were to reach these people. We knew that God was on the street and His heart ached for these people.

Once again, I found my own interests focusing on the issues of addiction. I found myself spending time with the alcoholics and drug users. It was time well spent as I learned so much during those days. The beginnings of what I teach these days come out of our time in Earls Court.

As time went on, the Earls Court team built a connection with Holy Trinity Brompton (HTB). A large Anglican church in the Kensington area of London just down the road from Harrods. One of the staff there was, in fact, the chaplain to Harrods. HTB is also the church that birthed the Alpha course which has gone on to be such a successful ministry worldwide.

AN ADVENTURE LIKE NO OTHER | *Warwick Murphy*

The connection with HTB was, in some ways, a strange one as many of the people from HTB were from the top end of town whereas the people we were dealing with in Earls Court were from the other end. However, it was a relationship that prospered and often people from HTB would join us in outreach in Earls Court.

At Christmas time we were offered the use of the basement at the YWCA at one end of Earls Court Rd. This was a big space and for two weeks over the Christmas period we used that space to meet many of the needs of the people we were working with. We had a space where people could get some new clothes. We had a couple of doctors who set up a small clinic for our clients, and every day we fed them a main meal. The highlight was the Christmas day meal. Harrods had offered to provide the food for this event. So here was the sight of these street people who normally survived on take away, or whatever else they could lay their hands on, sitting up at tables eating food from one of the best stores in London. I still get a smile when I think about it.

Working with these people brings you down to earth very quickly. There is no room for pride or self-aggrandizement. Street people see through those and will bring you back to reality in no time. Two situations taught me something about myself and the inability of governments to fully comprehend the problems in people's lives.

One morning, I was making my way to a meeting near South Kensington tube station. I was just another one of the thousands of people on their way to either work or school or somewhere else seemingly important. As I was walking through this crowd, I heard my name being called. I stopped, looked around, but could not see who was calling so I kept walking. Then I heard it again. Again, I looked around and then I saw him. John, one of our clients from Earls Court, which is just down the road from South Ken tube, sitting on someone's doorstep and calling my name. He was, it seemed, invisible to the passing crowd as they went about their business. Yet he was calling out my name in the hope that I, at

Chapter 12 Hitting the Streets

least, would acknowledge that he was there, and that he had some importance to someone. John was a chronic alcoholic and already at 9 a.m. was well under the weather, and he looked like it. His clothes were tattered and there was saliva and other unknown things spilling down his chin and running down his coat. His hair was filthy, and I had no doubt, even from where I was standing, that he would have had a certain stench about him.

For a few seconds I stood wondering if I could just keep walking and try to ignore him. But of course, I couldn't. So, I swallowed my pride and walked across the street and sat on the doorstep with him. He put his arm around me and told me how much he loved me. And yes, I was right about his smell. A mixture of alcohol and urine. I also knew that he had now blessed me with this same smell so that when I finally arrived at my meeting, they would know I had arrived before I walked through the door. It did mean though that I had a seat to myself. In God's eyes, John was just as important as all the rest of us going about our important business and he needed a friend. I have been around addictions long enough now to know that many addicted people are not no-hopers. Some have been professional doctors and dentists, some have been teachers. Please do not judge what you see on the outside. Every street person you see has a story as to why they are where they are.

The second story is about a guy who used to come into the coffee shop each week. We called him "Christmas tree Dave". He always had a strip of tinsel in his hair, a long beard, a guitar with no strings, and a bag full of we-knew-not-what. He had mental health issues and hardly spoke to anyone. He would sit on a chair, drink his tea, and just wanted to be near people. That was all we knew about him.

At one of our Christmas functions in the basement of the YWCA a man came up to me and said, *"Hello Warwick, how are you?"* I looked at him trying to think of where I had seen him before, but could not place him. Eventually he smiled and said, *"You don't know who I am do you?"* I apologized and replied, *"No, I don't."*

He continued smiling and said, *"I'm Christmas tree Dave."* I just stood there. I had no ideas what to say for some time while he just kept smiling.

Later, as I talked with him, he told us the story. He said he lived in a council flat not far from Earls Court. We had always thought he lived on the street. He told us that his flat had become full of rubbish and vermin and eventually the neighbours complained to the council. Finally, the council intervened. They put Dave in a hospital while they had a team come in and totally clean up his flat. While he was in the hospital, he was put on medication for his mental health issues and slowly became the gentleman I was talking to that evening. By now he was back in his flat and there was a district nurse giving him his medication each day. Dave was as lucid as anyone I had seen. He was clean and shaven, his hair was combed and neat. In short, he was a new man.

However, as time went on the funding for the regular visits from the nurse was stopped. Fairly quickly Dave reverted back to what we all knew him as. The last time I saw him the tinsel was back in the hair. He had found another guitar and he did not talk to us. As I write this I am still angry that this man is condemned to this life. I know governments try, and the health service in London did a great job, but they can never do it all. I have no idea what the answers are for people like Dave, but I keep meeting them and will continue to hope we find the answer one day.

HIV/Aids

Around this time the problem of AIDS hit the headlines. This was a new "disease" that had scientists looking for information. There were rumors abounding that it was God's judgement on homosexuals. There were rumors about how you could be infected with HIV if you drank out of the same cup as someone who had

Chapter 12 Hitting the Streets

the disease. In short, there was ignorance in the community, and indeed in the medical profession as well, about this situation. People were dying and no one really understood, or knew, why. Earls Court being at the heart of the homosexual community in London was seeing deaths every day. Due to the public ignorance, if it were known that there was someone with AIDS living somewhere, the people who collected the garbage each week would refuse to touch such a person's rubbish. Hospitals were isolating people, understandably. One doctor in particular, in London, was appalled by the way these people were treated. Dr. Patrick Dixon decided that as a Christian he could not continue to treat people in such a manner. At the time, AIDS was a terminal disease. If you had HIV there was a good prospect that you would contract AIDS and then die a lonely and sad death. Thank goodness we have seen much progress in our knowledge and understanding of this disease to the degree that today people with HIV have a great chance of leading a long and normal life.

Dr. Dixon realized that many of these people who were dying wanted to die at home, not in a hospital. Together with members from the Earls Court Team and HTB he pulled together the first AIDS Home Care team in London. June, as a trained nurse was very keen to get involved in this team. Her ability to connect with patients and people in desperate situations has been seen time and time again. It was a natural step for her to become a member of this team. They would go to the home of someone who was dying and look after them. Feed them, bathe them, and love them. June happened to be on duty with the team on the night the first patient died. June said it was such a privilege to talk and pray with this man in his last hours. They talked about life, family, and, of course, heaven. The aim of the team was not evangelical as such. They were there to love these people and serve them. But this service opened doors for deeper conversations. Working on this team was one of the highlights of our time in London for June. It was also on this team that we met a lady, Sue, who would eventually come and work with us in the rehab when we opened it.

Since that time, many other groups have become involved in working in this field, but I believe that Dr. Patrick Dixon is due much credit for his work of caring for people in this area and also for his work of education for the wider public. He has written a number of books on the subject of HIV/AIDS and is now a well-known speaker at many events attended by world leaders.

At times I found myself smiling as I recalled my background growing up in a wonderful average family in Sydney, and here I was spending my time with prostitutes, transsexuals, drug users, street sleepers, and alcoholics. This was practical Christianity, working with God on the streets and loving every minute of it. But every night we still had the same problem. We would go home, sometimes at 3 or 4 a.m. to a nice warm bed, and we knew that some of our new friends only had a cardboard box. The frustration continued.

Chapter 13

'The Chase'

While all this was happening, we had been put in touch with two wonderful old ladies who had a house in Clapham, just south of the Thames river, which they had run as a center for needy people. The house was situated on a road called the Chase, and over the years, the house had become known simply as "The Chase". The old ladies, Dr. Adams and Miss Whittaker, now lived in S.W. England and they had other people who ran the house for them. We had been made aware that they were looking for new people to run it. Could this be what we were looking for? Could this be why we had come to London? Could this be what we had been praying for?

June and I went and had a look at the house. It was the typical London house, one floor down and three up. It appeared to be in need of some repair, but it was ideal. Meetings were held between YWAM and the two ladies and finally agreement was reached that YWAM would take over the running of the house with June and me as house parents. It was hard to take in. Here was a house, four miles from the west end of London, being handed to us for no cost. The agreement was that the ladies would still own the house and we would keep them informed with our activities. The main concern of these Godly ladies was that the house would continue to be used to see God bring change to the lives of needy people.

AN ADVENTURE LIKE NO OTHER | *Warwick Murphy*

We were ready to move in! But it is never that easy when God is birthing something new. The family that was house sitting for the ladies decided that they were not moving out. They believed that this was their ministry, and they should stay. The ladies made it very clear to them that they could not stay but still they refused. The ladies offered them lovely accommodation elsewhere, but it was refused. It seemed that every day the situation became worse. June was in the final stages of pregnancy with our fourth child and the church manse we had been living in was needed for the new vicar. We started to feel like Joseph and Mary. After some weeks it became very apparent that these people were not going to move out voluntarily. They would need to be evicted. Thankfully, that was not our responsibility. Dr. Adams and Miss Whittaker found themselves in the terrible position of having to go through the courts to evict this family, and it was not a quick process. Because of the tenancy laws in England at the time it took another six months before the house was vacant.

By then, June had given birth to our fourth child, Elissa. Still no handbook though. One thing about having four children is that by the time the fourth comes along you are much more confident in being a parent and you also have older children who are happy to look after the new bundle of joy that she was, and still is. Having a first child changes so much in the life of a family. By the time Elissa arrived we felt a lot more comfortable and she just seemed to fit in. Not that she would have time to feel comfortable in this house in London.

Elissa's birth was fine, but June was very ill afterwards having halved her blood volume and needed much care for some months. She was in no condition to do much at all. Walking across a room was hard work. However, being part of an organization such as YWAM has benefits. YWAM had a large center in the midlands known as the King's Lodge. This is a large training facility situated on 16 acres and they had a vacant bungalow out the back. They were kind enough to offer us the use of this bungalow. We made

Chapter 13 'The Chase'

the move from teeming London to a rural property where we looked out our window on the dairy farm over the fence. The staff at the King's Lodge made us very welcome and in some ways we acted as pastors and counselors to many of the staff at the Lodge. Our two oldest children were enjoying attending the local school and our third child, Bryn, was making friends with many of the people at the Lodge, especially one of the young guys, Phillip. Bryn would follow Phillip all around the place and was always on the lookout for his friend, Phillip. As Elissa was a newborn, we had no end of people wanting to babysit which was also very helpful as June did not have enough strength to look after her all the time. The King's Lodge was a real haven for our family, and we are eternally grateful for their kindness.

Once again, the emotions were in turmoil. Having prepared ourselves to the point of setting up a new ministry, suddenly it was snatched away. Having become excited about the prospect of finally doing what we had gone to England for, here we were in the country not knowing how long we would have to wait. While June recovered and our two older children attended a local school, I drove a ride on a mower for six months and trapped moles. Initially, frustration was a big problem, but it did not take long to learn to enjoy our situation. Looking back, I think we really needed this break before opening the doors on a very demanding work. However, there is always something else to learn with God. As I sat on the mower each day, I found my prayers were based in anger at the situation we were in rather than in compassion. I felt that we had lost a spiritual battle over the Chase and I expected God to move on our behalf to bring a righteous result. It still amazes me to know how quickly we can revert to seeing our situation as the most important thing on God's agenda. Our arrogance is enormous. No wonder God calls us to humility.

In His mercy, God allowed me to continue to pray this way until one day I stopped and decided that maybe I should wait on Him to see if He had anything to say on the matter. How good of me to condone to let God direct my prayers, to think that maybe He may want some input! Needless to say, God had much to say, although it was very different to what I had expected. He made it very clear to me that He was in no hurry to get us into the Chase. He was more concerned for the family I had been praying against. The family who I believed had stopped us from doing God's will. I sensed God's heart of compassion for this family. I began to realize that it was not all about me and my selfish attitudes. He was concerned for them as well and He showed me that I needed to change my attitude and begin to bring my praying into line with His purposes. I needed to pray from a heart of compassion for this family. Another lesson learned, hopefully.

As is often the case in these circumstances, once I had sought out God's way of doing things He then moved. At long last the legal saga was over. The family in the Chase was legally evicted from the property, and had somewhere else to live, and we were able to make the move back to London and begin a work that we believed would change the lives of hurting people, and in the process change us as well.

During our time at The King's Lodge, we had met a few people who had expressed a desire to join our team at the Chase. Martin was a young man with some musical and leadership abilities. Sue was a young Australian woman with a big heart for drug users. Both had been through YWAM DTS and were keen to get their hands dirty. We all moved into the house around the same time. We wanted time to get to know each other and pray about the direction ahead. The vagueness of the original dream, to open a house for hurting people, now needed to have structure and detail added. The only thing we really knew how to do was pray, so that was where we started. We felt that this was a new beginning for this house. We were not to be just another group of people running what had run before. It was time to develop something new. The truth was that we had the vision to do something but little understanding of how to do it. We were all flying by the seat of our pants.

Chapter 14

In at the Deep End

It was not long before the phone was ringing with people wanting to move in as residents. As we had to house staff in the house, plus our family, we could only take a maximum of six residents at a time. It did not take long for those beds to fill up. After a few weeks at one of our staff meetings, someone mentioned that every one of our residents had a drug or alcohol problem. Then Sue, one of our staff, said she had a confession to make. She said that she had been praying that the Chase would become a residential drug rehabilitation center. In some ways we had no choice as we needed to work with our residents to overcome their drug problem.

This was where our real training in addictions began in earnest. Living with addicts is like moving from studying at High School to University. Except that this university was to do with people's lives. The learning curve was steep, to say the least.

The basic program that we put in place was that a resident would commit to stay for 12 months. Through that time they would work their way through a three-phase program, looking at a number of issues around addiction. The drivers of addiction, the triggers of addiction, relapse and relapse prevention, forgiveness and restitution. We also realized that we could do as much teaching as we liked but there were other issues that needed to change in the lives of our residents. These things came to light in various ways. It is interesting to note at this point that, although each resident was given time with a staff member each week for counseling, we learned more about these people in our general living situations.

Some of our residents were attending Narcotics Anonymous meetings regularly, and one evening Jerry, one of our residents, had just returned from an NA meeting and was making a cup of tea in the kitchen when we started talking. He suddenly said to me, *"You Christians don't like lust do you?"* I was a bit surprised at his question, but did not want to miss this opportunity, so I started talking to him about lust. Eventually I asked him why he had asked, and he said, *"Well, I have been thinking about becoming a Christian, but giving up my lust would be a problem for me because I really enjoy my lust."* You won't hear that statement in too many churches. There followed a conversation about the connection between lust, the abuse of women, and respect for women.

On another occasion I was watching the evening news with this same guy when a report came through that a police officer had just been killed during a riot in North London. Jerry jumped up on the couch and started shouting, *"Yes, Yes, Yes."* The anger and violence in his voice took me totally by surprise. It was moments such as this that showed us that there were issues in these people's lives that we had not expected, or even thought about addressing. We needed to rethink a few things.

This type of thing drives you to pray. Every day we were aware of our limitations, but we were keen to learn how to bring change into a damaged life. We could either ignore some of this stuff and just carry on with the program we had, or we could find some answers. In the Bible, we are told in the book of Romans, chapter 12, that we can be transformed by the renewing of our minds and this will lead us to God's will for our lives. We felt it was time to confront some of these issues that were floating to the surface, but in a different way. We could just talk to the residents about these things, but

Chapter 14 In at the Deep End

we knew this could go in one ear and out the other. They needed practical help to learn. We needed to tweak the program.

Even though we had two women on the staff, June was very much seen as the mother of the house, and Sue was quite a strong person in her own right. About this time, we had an application to join the staff from a young Canadian girl, Heidi. After praying and interviewing her, we felt she should join us. Heidi was a very attractive young woman with long curly hair and with her Canadian accent it just seemed to add to her attractiveness with the residents. I think almost every guy we had staying with us while Heidi was there fell in love with her. Although this was tough on Heidi, she helped us to show the residents that women were more than sex objects or people to do their bidding. They could carry authority and should be dealt with from a point of respect. We were confronting a deep-seated belief in the lives of these guys. It is interesting to note that every male addict we have ever dealt with has what we call a codependent woman somewhere in their lives. This may be their mother, sister, girlfriend, or wife, who enables these people to continue their addictive lifestyle. They don't mean to assist the addiction, but their actions do exactly that. They continue to clean up after them. They pay outstanding bills. They run errands for them. All of this enables the addict to continue in their lifestyle without suffering too many bad consequences. Why would they need to change when they don't have to do much? Most of us learn the lessons of life by making mistakes and then having to pay the price of that mistake. Eventually we learn that bad consequences have a big price, and then we start to alter our behavior, initially to avoid the consequences before learning that doing the right thing makes life a lot easier. The codependent person in the addict's life stops these people from learning this valuable life lesson. I understand that they do it because they are trying to save the life of their loved one, but they are also creating a burden for themselves that the addict will gladly let them bear. Having said that, I, in no way, make a judgement on these people. It is easy for me to tell them to stop assisting the addiction. But the situation for a mother who has a son telling her that if she does not give him what he wants at that time then he will go out and overdose and if he dies it will be all her fault, this is a terrible place for that lady to find herself in. I cannot imagine the internal wrestling that these people go through on a daily basis.

One funny, but sad, side effect of this time must be mentioned. One of the guys who had been with us for some time was allowed to go out of the house on his own, however on this one occasion he obviously had managed to purchase some drugs while out and when he arrived home, just in time for dinner, he was obviously high. He sat at the table trying to hide his situation while we all could easily see what he was trying to hide. He piled his plate with a great mound of mashed potatoes and by now the drugs were taking full effect and he was about to pass out. He looked across the table at Heidi, and as his head drooped towards the mashed potatoes, he declared his undying love for her and asked her to marry him. We could not help ourselves and the laughter was very loud. June was the one to show some compassion and had managed to grab his head just before it ended up in the potatoes. We all then received a small lecture from June about our behavior. However, it was moments like these that enabled us as parents to our own children to explain to them the side of drug use that most kids never see.

Another issue that needed addressing was the issue of authority. We were learning that addicts don't like authority figures. For an addict, authority figures are simply people who will not let them have their own way. They don't like being told what to do, and they like to think that they are the ones who should be in control, and they mostly see the police as the worst authority figure in their lives. As it happened around this time, we had a visit from a local police officer. He had heard about our work and wanted to know more about it. He was a young Christian guy and so I invited him to come back in a few days' time to share a meal with us all. I particularly asked him to wear his uniform and explained why. He was a bit surprised, but said he would. We told the guys we

Chapter 14 In at the Deep End

would be having a visitor for lunch but did not mention that he was a police officer. They were keen to meet someone new so when he walked in, in uniform, you could have cut the air with a knife. I think if we had not been there they would have told him just what they thought of him and the rest of the police force.

The staff and I just kept having a normal conversation with him and eventually some of the guys couldn't help themselves and bought into the conversation as well. They had calmed down enough to frame their questions with some politeness and the officer was happy to engage their questions and try to explain a police officer's view of things. It turned out to be a very positive time and I believe helped some of them to move on in their views.

We also took the residents to the National Gallery in Trafalgar Square. Interestingly, most of these guys had lived in London for years and never been to any of these famous places, such as the National Gallery, or the wonderful museums that can be found in London. Some of the guys thought this was a total waste of time, but others were surprised at how much they enjoyed this whole new world. After that excursion, a number of them started drawing when they arrived back home and some of their work was not too bad. They had never seen that they might have a talent in some of these areas. We have learned over the years that many of the people we have worked with have talents in the arts, business, sport, etc. Why? Because they are no different than anyone else, it is just that no one has ever opened that door in their lives.

Chapter 15

Family in the rehab

While we were learning about the field of addiction, we were also raising our children in a drug rehabilitation center. At the time, it just seemed so normal to do that. Although I am sure Dr. Spock would have frowned upon the idea, we believe it was the right thing to do, for our family, at that time. It enabled two things to happen. Firstly, it allowed our children to see the side of addiction that not many children get to see. The issue with the mashed potatoes, which I mentioned earlier, gave us a platform to explain to our children that this was a side of drug use that people rarely see. A person made to look silly and the butt of everyone else's humor. We spoke very openly with our kids about these things as they grew up. We were also very careful to keep an eye on them and had boundaries about residents not being allowed into our part of the facility. The kids needed to know that our space was safe and private.

The other thing we learned through watching the resident's interaction with our children was that these people were immature. We were learning that when someone starts to use drugs on a regular basis they stop maturing emotionally. Many of the residents related easily with our kids because in effect they were still kids themselves. The problem for them is that the addict may be a 25-year-old man, with all the expectation of being treated as such, but their behavior is just like a young child. Hence the tantrums,

Chapter 15 Family in the rehab

etc., if they don't get their own way. Except a tantrum for a 25-year-old looks like anger and can result in violence.

I am sure that our children have mixed views about this period in their lives and may tell a slightly different story but that will be for a book that they may write. However, June was in her element. Being an extrovert, she thrived having so many people around us. She also thrived in ministry. June has a spiritual awareness that came to the fore in this house. Praying for our guys. Confronting them when necessary and generally being mum in the house. We did not know just how much these guys respected her until one night one of our former residents phoned late at night. He had been arrested and the only person he thought to phone and ask for help was June. We went to the police station and managed to see him home that night. He knew June would act and make something happen.

The things we were learning at the Chase have been the foundation of much of the teaching we do these days.

Chapter 16
The 'Mish'

As with most like minded groups of people, addicts tend to gather in groups and build their community with these same people. Think of various ethnic groups that migrate to other countries. For obvious reasons these people live near each other and set up shops that sell products that they are familiar with, etc. It is this activity that creates the "Chinatowns" that we find in most western cities today. Addicts do the same thing. Their common interest draws them together. They share information on dealers, who has the best "gear", where the best squat is, and more.

To counter this mindset, we felt strongly that we needed to introduce our residents to a whole new set of people. This is easier said than done. Not everyone wants to associate with addicts, whether they are in recovery or not. People have genuine concerns about whether these people will influence their children or steal their belongings. We needed to tread carefully here.

Part of the program in the house was to attend church every Sunday. This was explained to each prospective resident when they came for an interview. The reason for this rule was more about introducing our residents to a whole new group of people than about seeing them give consideration to their spiritual life. Our family had been attending a little fellowship situated at the bottom of a group of tower blocks in Battersea. This church was part of the Shaftesbury

Chapter 16 The 'Mish'

Society, and one of several churches they had planted many years before. It was simply known then, and to this day, as "The Mish", short for the Shaftesbury Mission. The members of this church were a wonderful eclectic mix of people. Some from the tower blocks, some from a little further afield. Some living on welfare, some with well-paying jobs. All committed to developing a church that would reach the people in the area and excited to spread the Gospel in the area.

The pastor of this church was Tony Powell. He was ably assisted by his wife, Ruth, and an excellent leadership team. This group of people welcomed us, as a family, into their church and were keen to find out what a family of Australians was doing in this area. Once we explained about the Chase, this church was keen to get involved. I cannot speak too highly about this group of people. They accepted the residents of the Chase into their midst. Various church members would invite some of our residents home for lunch on Sunday after church, or indeed on family outings to the park, etc. In short, they reached out beyond their comfort zone and embraced these young men in a way that our residents had never experienced before. This church truly exhibited the love and acceptance of God to people who previously would have expected rejection and a sense of being excluded.

I have to say that this church was rare in this regard. I have seen, and heard, of churches that have wanted to reach out to struggling people only to find that it is never what they expected. The Shaftesbury fellowship managed to bridge the gap in a way that I had not seen before. I believe a lot of this was due to the pastor and his wife. Tony became a very close friend to me personally and he is a man that I respect greatly. There are no bells and whistles with Tony. He is the genuine article and a natural-born pastor. It was during this time that we had received word that my nephew in Australia, Shaughan, had been killed in what looked like an accident, but there were also thoughts as to whether he had actually committed suicide. Recall that at this time there was no internet, just phone calls and letters. I had been there when Shaughan was born. I loved this kid deeply. He was 21 when he died. I was in a state of shock. I was devastated. I had pastored people through times like this. I knew all the things that should be said, but it made no difference to the pain I felt. I sat in our lounge room and wept. June was wise enough to call Pastor Tony. He came straight away and did the most amazing thing. He came into the lounge room and just sat next to me. He didn't say anything at all for a long time. He just sat there, in silence, holding me. I did not want anyone speaking clichés to me. In many ways I did not want anyone saying anything at all. My grief was so raw. Tony's actions that day was all that I needed. Just another person, another heartbeat, to sit there in silence. Tony is one of the most naturally gifted pastors I have ever come across and it showed in the people in his church. He retired from the work in Battersea many years back now but is still a pastor to many people. The church in Battersea has continued under the leadership of Brian and Jo Watts, people Tony and his wife, Ruth, had discipled.

From this relationship with the Mish we learned that, although we lived in the house with our residents on a daily basis, successful recovery needed more than just us. We also realized that we, as staff, needed a wider scope in our lives. Most, if not all, addicts believe that they can overcome their addiction all by themselves. The truth is that they cannot. Many rehabs believe that they can also do it all on their own. Once again, the truth is that they cannot. We all need others to help us through this life.

Growth in our understanding of this work.

However, the truth was that at the beginning we really had little idea of actually what to do with our guests at the Chase. Having a desire to help people in need, having somewhere to provide housing and food for them, and having staff who also wanted to help all mean very little when it comes down to the day-to-day issues. Good intentions are not enough.

Chapter 16 The 'Mish'

People have asked me how we came to work with drug addicts? The short answer is "by accident". The real answer is because that was what God wanted us to do.

One thing I have often said about drug users is that they are honest with you. They may be dishonest in many ways but when it comes to letting you know where you stand with them, they are brutally honest.

We quickly grew to love these guys. I could write another book with the stories of each of them and our dealings in their lives, but that is for another time. To say that our lives changed from then on would be a gross understatement. We would never be the same again. Here we were a family with four young children living in a house with a bunch of drug addicts. What parents would do that? We learned more about people with problems, about ourselves, about God's heart for people, than we could ever have done through a specific educational course or theology course. The learning curve was steep but neither June nor I would have had it any other way. As an example, we had decided that for one week we would teach about family. Every morning we had a time in the house for teaching, or discussion, or both. Knowing that these guys had come from tough backgrounds we thought some teaching on family could be helpful. If this sounds patronizing that was exactly what it was. We, the staff were the experts, and they were the poor souls who needed to learn from the experts.

So, the first morning I had been speaking for some time about "family" when one of the residents spoke up and said, **"Warwick, I have no idea what you are talking about."** This threw me because I thought I was doing an OK job explaining family. So, I asked him, **"What do you think family is?"** He then started to talk about what was obviously his experience of family. He talked about living in a council house with his mum and siblings, He talked about the number of different men who came and went through their lives. He could not talk about his father because he had left before he knew him. He went on for some time and I noticed the other guys in the room nodding in agreement with his take on what a family looked like. Guess who learned the most that day? We had to reshape our program, but once again we had learned how seemingly ill-equipped, we were for this role.

We were fortunate to have good people around us to support us and who had some idea of the issues we were wrestling with. This was where we were meant to be and there is a peace deep inside that assures you of that very thing.

People with drug or alcohol issues are manipulative, they lie, they dislike authority, and they are extremely self-centered. Having said all that, they can be some of the most loyal people if they see that you are trying to help them. Every day at the Chase was an adventure. A roller coaster of emotions and learning. There were hard times and there were very funny times. We cried and we laughed with these guys who were growing into our hearts. Living our faith out in front of these guys was a joy. They had so many questions as to why we did certain things. Why did we discipline our children? Why did we pray? How could God love people like them? We saw a number of them baptized at the Mish and I was best man at one of their weddings.

One of the things that happened while we were learning was that I was being asked to speak at various places on the issue of addiction. In other words, I was being seen as some sort of expert on drugs. I have to say that I was no expert. Even today I do not consider myself an expert. I have some expertise in the addiction field, but there is still much more to learn. We were still learning but we did have more of an understanding than some. One of these invitations turned out to be a very funny evening. One group, attached to a rather large church in London, had been working on plans to develop a recovery work in Africa. They had come to visit us at the Chase and as they were leaving, they said that they would be having a dedication service in a few weeks' time and would

Chapter 16 The 'Mish'

I be the guest speaker for the evening. Wanting to encourage others in this ministry, I accepted their invitation. On the given night, June and I arrived at this church to find a large crowd of people gathering and a long table set up on the platform for important guests. The evening began with a prayer and then the important guests were introduced. I was introduced as Dr. Warwick Murphy, the expert in residential rehabilitation. June and I just looked at each other as there was no way to correct him. I had been asked to speak for around 20 minutes and had prepared accordingly. Prior to my speaking, numerous people were asked to pray or introduce themselves. All the others at the table on the platform were Africans. There were bishops and pastors, etc. Without being rude here if you have ever been to an African church you will know that they like to pray and speak for a long time. This evening was no different. As each person prayed or shared, they seemed to take longer than the previous one, and knowing that we had to vacate the premises by 10:30 p.m., I began to wonder when they would get to me. Eventually the host leaned over to me and whispered in my ear, asking if I could cut my speaking time down a few minutes. I was fine with that and then more long prayers and speeches. Eventually the host leaned over again and, looking totally embarrassed, said to me, *"I am sorry, but we will not have time for your speech."* I was the guest speaker, but there was no time for me to speak. June and I have laughed about this event many times.

During this time, we had heard about another Christian rehabilitation center based in Reading, just outside London. All the reports we had heard about Yeldall Manor were very positive so we decided that it would be good to see this work and meet the team running it. After phoning and arranging an appropriate date we traveled out there to find a large facility which looked to me like an old Manor House. The director, David Partington, came out to meet us and generously gave us of his time to talk about the work of Yeldall. I actually don't remember much of what the conversation was about, but I have never forgotten Dave. At the time he seemed very businesslike but over the years I have come to know, and appreciate, a man of humility, wisdom, and humor. Dave is a man who has that rare ability of making a person feel that they are the most important person in the world when they are talking to him. My connection and respect for Dave just continued to grow over the years and I have no hesitation in saying that I love this man dearly. He has been a voice of reason in my life for many years now and indeed has been instrumental in opening the doors to what we are now doing in Asia as I write this book.

God brings saints and angels through our lives and many times I think we miss their importance until we look back years later. Writing this book has been helpful in recalling some of the saints and angels that have passed through my life. You will meet them as you read.

Chapter 17

Renovations

Although good things were happening in the lives of everyone living at the Chase the building itself was badly in need of repair. Literally, patch up jobs had been the story of this building for many years. We were only made aware of how bad it was later when a building survey was done, but more of that later.

It was a visit from the pastor of the little Shaftesbury fellowship we were attending that precipitated something far beyond my expectations. In conversation with Tony the state of the building came up in discussion. I explained that I had no idea of how much any renovations would cost or even where to begin as the building was still owned by the two godly women living in Bodmin. Tony suggested that the Shaftesbury Society may be able to do something. The Shaftesbury Society is a charitable organization established by Lord Shaftesbury in the nineteenth century and, by the 1980s, they were running many facilities to assist struggling people in London as well as having also planted several churches around London.

After some discussion, Tony said he would take our situation to this organization to see how they could help. Within a short time, two men from the society were on the doorstep wanting to talk about how they could help. After a tour of the building and learning something of its history they said they would draw up a proposal and present to us. At this stage I was encouraged that something might happen and that we might be able to do some repainting and a few other minor repairs on the building.

Weeks later these two men arranged to come by to present their proposal to us. So, there we sat in my office. Tony Powell, myself, and the two men from the Shaftesbury Society. They produced a large document containing a proposal to purchase and renovate the entire property. I had no idea they were thinking so broadly. I am sure my lower jaw could be seen on the carpet.

After I had composed myself, I asked the question, **"What would that cost and where would you get the money?"** Remember this building was only four miles from the west end of London. Houses around us were expensive, let alone the cost of repair. One of the men looked at me and said, **"I believe that we can get a grant from the government to cover it all. Probably in the realm of 500,000 pounds."** At the time that was more than $ 1.2 million. I could not believe what I was hearing. There is a lot more detail to this episode than I will add here but eventually the building was sold to the Society and the complete renovation of this building was done. When the engineers came to survey what had to be done they were amazed that no-one had fallen through the floors because the house was full of dry rot. The rebuilding entailed basically taking the old structure down, leaving the front facade, and building again. After the building was finished, the Shaftesbury Society then provided the funds to totally refurnish the house as well. We were going to get a brand-new facility, plus all the furnishings. Wow. However, it also meant that our family would need to move out of the house while the rebuilding was done, but also once it was finished, we could not live there again. Because we were caring for people in need the government had certain regulations about how the building could be constructed. In light of this we would need to find another house for our family.

The Shaftesbury Society gave us a rough idea of how much we could spend on a house, so we started looking. House prices in

Chapter 17 Renovations

London are not cheap and the more we looked the further away from the Chase we seemed to get. It truly seemed like an impossible task. To summarize. We were going to get a new building, new furnishings, and another house for the directors to live in. All without having to do a fund-raising campaign. This was God's provision as only He can do it.

Chapter 18

Trip home

We had felt the Lord show us that this was the ideal time to head back to Australia for a much-needed furlough. We had been told that the rebuilding would take at least six months, so we set about planning the trip. There are two ways to travel to Australia from the UK, via Asia or via the US. Then we realized that there was another option. An around the world ticket. Friends of ours were working with addicts in Karachi, Pakistan and had invited us to visit if at all possible. As we talked about it, we thought of friends all around the world. Being a part of a mission organizations like YWAM means you end up with many friends all over the place. In talking to a travel agent, we found that the round-the-world ticket would be ideal for us and was in fact cheaper than the other options. However, the term "cheaper" is a very relative term. There were six of us and we knew this trip was going to cost a lot of money, which we did not have. YWAM people do not receive a wage. Everyone in YWAM from the top down are trusting God for their finances. So, although we had worked in London for some years, we had no funds to fall back on. This was going to be a huge faith challenge. This was not a new pair of shoes I needed. We needed thousands of pounds. We prayed. At times like this it is important to know whether God is with you in the challenge. We needed something to indicate to us whether God was in this plan. We quickly realized that we would need new passports. So, we brought that before the Lord in prayer. Within days of praying we received a financial gift from someone we had

Chapter 18 Trip home

only met once. This person had never supported us financially before, and never since. The amount of the gift he sent was exactly the amount, to the penny, that we needed for new passports. I looked at June and said, *"Well, we are going somewhere."* Against the whole amount that we needed this gift was small, but it was the catalyst for the faith that we needed to see the rest of the money come in. Sometimes you just need a small thing to build your faith upon. This was that small thing. This was like a faith seed. When that gift arrived in the mail, my faith just rose. I knew this was God confirming that we were to take on this challenge.

Trusting God in these types of faith challenges means stepping out of our comfort zone and doing practical things toward the end goal. When Moses and the children of Israel stood at the edge of the Red Sea, Moses told the people to prepare to cross to the other side. The sea was still in front of them, but he told them to be ready to move. When Jesus fed the five thousand, He told the disciples to get the people to sit down in preparation for being fed. He still only had five loaves and two fish in front of Him. We felt that we needed to be living like we were heading back to Australia. We also knew that this was a faith challenge such as we had not engaged in before. So, we put the TV away and focused our time on the challenge. Prayer, and at times fasting. As few distractions as possible to the challenge. Then we started packing up the house in readiness to move.

Eventually the day came when we realized that we needed to book tickets. I must say that I had been putting this off for some time. I found a travel agent in London, went in and told them what we needed. The man spent time on the computer looking through the options and finally decided on a route that would take us to Karachi, Bangkok, Perth, Melbourne (where we spent six months), then on to New Zealand, Hawaii, and Los Angeles. We had decided it was possible to catch a train across the US and fly out from New York back to London. So, the tickets we booked took us to the west coast of the US plus the train across the States. I asked the agent the cost of all this and I managed to stay upright when he told me. I asked if I could put a deposit down. He said yes, they would need at least 200 pounds as a deposit and the balance in two weeks. I had 200 pounds on me, paid the deposit and left, assuring the man I would be back with the rest in two weeks. As I walked out of his office, I thought to myself, "If he only knew that I had just paid him with the last 200 pounds to our name, he would never have accepted that we could pay the rest." We were taking steps in faith. If God has said He will do something, then we should be able to move forward believing and acting in a manner that says we will see what God has said will come to pass. Hebrews 11 is all about this. In fact, the history of the Church is just this. People who have heard God lead them on to something and move in such a way that they expect to see what their eyes cannot see at that moment. Faith is not sitting, waiting for everything to be in place before action. It is stepping out, confident that it will happen. It is interesting to note that when Jesus healed people, He quite often made them "do" something. A blind man had to go and wash his eyes in a certain pool. A bedridden man had to make the effort to get up before the healing took place. We must be confident in God to the extent that we will move forward in expectation. Following are a few steps that need following when we step out in faith.

- Hearing God speak to you about a particular thing.
- Confirming that it is from God.
- Continuous prayer.
- Believing that God will do what He has said.
- Stepping out in confidence toward the goal.
- Putting your hand in your own pocket first.
- Reminding yourself of what God said when the doubts come and choosing to believe that God is faithful to His word.

This was the biggest faith challenge we had ever taken on and yet we were full of faith that we would see God do the miracle. We

Chapter 18 Trip home

believe that God gave us a gift of faith through this time. As those two weeks passed, we saw bits of money come in toward the trip, but we still were far short. On the last couple of days, while tension was building, a young couple came to us, saying they had felt God leading them to provide a large amount toward this challenge. That large amount was all the money we needed to enable me to walk into the travel agent's office on the appointed day and pay the balance that we owed. Were we excited? You bet we were. Yes, excited that we would be heading back to Australia to see family, but more excited that we had just seen God do a miracle.

The day finally came to leave on furlough. We had packed up the house, handed over the keys to the Shaftesbury Society and headed to the airport. At this stage, we still had not found a place for us to return to.

We flew out of Heathrow on Pakistani International Airways (PIA), or as some would have it "Perhaps It'll Arrive". We landed in Karachi, Pakistan, to be met by our friend, Phil Simpson, and a friend with two vehicles, which were needed to carry all of us plus our luggage. This was our first real taste of Asia. We had been through Asian airports before, but never spent any actual time in Asia. Karachi was a shock to the system. Everywhere we looked there were people. There seemed to be no space where there was no one. The traffic seemed to operate on its own rules. Cars and motorbikes went wherever. Whole families were on one bike. This was culture shock indeed.

Phil and his wife Rachel were working with the Church Missionary Society (CMS). They were working with addicts in Karachi and here we found a different way of doing things. There was no residential facility, Phil would visit the addicts in their homes and what I found interesting was that the whole family would sit in on the visit. They wanted to know what they could do, but also this was normal custom here. While we were used to working with young people in the main, here we found a much older group of addicts as well. Heroin was so cheap and easily obtained. The problem seemed huge. Phil and his wife, Rachel, looked after us so well. Eventually they, along with others, set up an organization called IBTIDA. This organization is still running and now has a residential facility.

We were confronted with so many new things in Karachi it is hard to describe. We must have looked like wide-eyed tourists during our 10 days there. However, it left an imprint that has never gone away, and today we find we are still in touch with people there and visiting Pakistan is part of what we do today. Indeed, it seemed that God planted something in our hearts for this part of the world, and Pakistan in particular. That plant would grow and bear fruit many years later.

From Karachi we traveled to Bangkok, Thailand. This was a great few days for the family, who managed to see some of this great city, but I had picked up something in Karachi that meant I needed to be very close to a toilet for some days. So, while the family looked around Bangkok, I spent the time in bed. The reason we were in Bangkok was that YWAM had a base there and their focus was working with the refugees coming out of Cambodia. Due to my illness, I never did get to see any of that work. The next stop was Perth in Australia. I was booked in as the speaker at the DTS there although I was still not completely over the case of "Delhi Belly" that I had picked up. From there it was onto Melbourne where we were to spend the bulk of the next six months.

This was a time of refreshing for us all. The church had found a nice house for us to rent while we were home, and the kids went to a local school. We spent much time with the wider family in Melbourne and made a few trips to Sydney to visit my family as well. It was indeed nice to be home.

Six months seemed to go very quickly though and soon enough we were back on a plane, this time to New Zealand. What a great country? Beaches, hot springs, and friends that we had worked with

Chapter 18 Trip home

in England. It was so good to catch up with people after some time and recall the events that we all lived and worked through.

From there, it was on to the YWAM base in Kona, Hawaii. We had heard much about this base, so it was good to finally see it up close. The base in Hawaii has a vision for reaching out to the Asia/Pacific region. It is also the main campus for the University of the Nations. An amazing center. As soon as you mention Hawaii images of palm trees and beaches come to mind. These things can easily be found there, but that is not the purpose of those working on the YWAM base. It is a training base for teams heading out to the Asia Pacific region.

Leaving there we headed to Los Angeles. YWAM had a work in Hollywood reaching out to the street people. Many of these young people had come to LA seeking their fortune in the movies. So many sad cases. So many expected that they would be "discovered" and their lives would suddenly change. They had bought into the dream that Hollywood presents. They had not realized that it *was* a dream. A fairy tale. These young people that we met there reminded me of the young people we would meet in the west end of London. Believing the lie that somewhere within those bright lights their lives would change. That all the pain that had caused them to leave home would disappear. That the attention and respect that they craved would heal the deep ache in their hearts. Instead, they found themselves living on the streets. Rejected by this city that had held out so many promises to them. The silver screen had collapsed and behind it all they found were the pimps and chancers that feed on people like them.

The couple who ran the work there are Joe and Trish Appler. They had previously visited us in London, so it was good to see the day-to-day workings of what they were doing. We have much regard for this couple and their family. We loved being with them and seeing the ministry there, and we still hold them as very dear friends. This couple had worked in similar fields to us but in different places in the world. They were committed to bringing the message of life to these young people. More saints and angels?

In LA, we had come to the end of our plane stops. Our plan was to catch the train across the US, which is what we did. Three days of an ever-changing landscape with a change of trains in Chicago, then on to New York. The last part of this trip to New York was one we prefer to forget. It seemed like one problem after another. We arrived at New York Central Station and I think we stepped into another world. I had heard about how New Yorkers can be rude, but after the great time we had had with people in LA, this was a shock. We had not planned to stay in New York, so we made our way to the airport.

For reasons that escape me now, when we planned the trip we had not built in a flight from New York to London, and we did not have the ready cash needed to get on a plane. Back in London, I had received an application for an American Express credit card. Knowing our financial situation would mean they would never accept me as a customer, I filled in the forms anyway and days later received a letter refusing my application. Much as I had expected. A few more days later and an American Express card arrived in the mail. We had a good laugh about it, and I put it in my wallet and forgot about it. Now sitting at the airport in New York, I realized that I could use the card to purchase tickets back to London. However, I did not want to presume that this was the right thing to do, so as a family we found a bit of space where we could pray about what we should do. Should we look up friends in New York and stay there while we sort out how to get back to London, or should we use the card and book the flights. After praying and waiting on God, we asked the kids what they felt we should do. Every one of us felt we should use the card. So, I booked six seats on a flight back to Heathrow, wondering how I was going to pay off the card, I must admit. To finalize this little story, not long after arriving back in London we had a message from our church back in Melbourne. They had taken up an offering for us the last Sunday before we left but had not had time to get the funds to us. Yes, the amount of that collection was the exact

Chapter 18 Trip home

amount of our airfares from New York. We were able to pay the credit card off. We were home again.

So, what was this trip all about. There were, in fact, a number of things that God was doing in our lives through this time. We learned far more about God's faithfulness regarding His provision. We were exposed to a much bigger picture of what God was doing in the area of addictions in YWAM. Thirdly, as we have looked back in later years, we can see that this trip also broadened our knowledge on what it is to work with the tough cases of people lost in the world of addiction. My friend, David Partington, often says that working in the ministry of addictions is one of the toughest areas of ministry that there is. Seeing how others were dealing with addictions and poverty in a variety of different cultures taught us much that is now being put to use.

As I related earlier, when we left London we had no idea where we would return to as we had not been able to find a suitable place that was close to the Chase. However, while we were away, our good friends Richard and Michelle Lahey James, more saints and angels, who headed up the Earls Court team, had been overseeing things with the Shaftesbury Society and the rebuild of the house while we were away from London. They had discussion with the society about our housing and finally they came to an agreement and found an amazing house within an easy walk from the Chase. It was a four-bedroom house with a backyard and parking. We were amazed. To find such a place in Battersea, London, was amazing. In fact, more than amazing. We had left London six months earlier where we had been living in what were actually quite cramped quarters for a family of six and had now returned to a four-bedroom house with a sizable backyard for London. We were thrilled. The Shaftesbury Society had bent over backwards to work with us through the renovating of the Chase and finding accommodation for us that was not too far from the ministry center. God's provision comes in many ways and I can only say that "thanks" is too little a way to express our gratitude for all that was taking place in this ministry.

Chapter 19

Frustrations

Although we had come back to a wonderful accommodation for our family, we had also expected to come back to a totally renovated house for the work. To our dismay, this was not the case. In fact, due to the new fire and building regulations that were needed to be adhered to for a facility such as the Chase, it meant that the design had to be altered and this involved architects, council officers, the fire department, etc. When we arrived back in London after those six months, the Chase looked much the same as when we had left.

We had come back to London with the expectation of working in the rehab. That was not possible now. What to do?

Walking a path with God is always so interesting. He only lets us see a short way up the road. At this point, I was frustrated that the building had hardly advanced over six months. I was annoyed at the delay and the reasons for it. I just wanted to get on with the work. However, we cannot achieve much by living in frustration. I needed to do something. YWAM London had several teams working in various parts around London, one of them was the team I had mentioned earlier that was based in Earls Court. By now this team was well established with some very good people onboard. They were happy for me to get involved. So, I became the team drug and alcohol worker, as well as being involved in the street outreach on several nights each week.

Chapter 19 Frustrations

So now June and I had involvement in Earls Court and with the building of the Chase. I know that June would have loved to have had more involvement in the work in Earls Court, but we also had four children that needed all the usual things that children need: relationships, transport to school, meals, attention, discipline. In short, love. June was also involved in the school that three of our children attended, so she was quite busy. Her involvement in the décor of the new rehab was also a time-consuming affair.

Care in the Community, etc.

As I have looked at church history down through the ages, I have noticed that it is rare that God rebuilds an old vision. It seems to me that He creates something new. The Reformation was not about rebuilding a corrupt church. It was about creating something new. The revivals in Britain in the 18th and 19th centuries were not about reviving a church that had become so out of touch with the community, a church that seemed to have lost touch with its purpose. These revivals were about creating something new. There were movements away from the dominant Anglican church. The Methodist church was born. Within a generation or two, the Methodist church needed refreshing again and we saw the birth of the Salvation Army. And so, it has been, and I believe always will be, and a whole book could be written on that subject alone.

In our situation in London, we were not rebuilding a church, but we needed to refresh the vision of what we were doing as well. We had pioneered the work, but now it needed a firmer structure. Again, history teaches us that pioneers go in and break the ground and establish a work, or indeed a city. History also shows us that there comes a time when what may be called "the Settlers" come into these new areas and they go on to build on the foundations that the pioneers have laid. In our case, we were seeing a new thing. Whereas before we had lived on site, now we were living away from the rehab. We needed new staff as well. With all this we felt it was time to give the work a new name too.

We called it Beth Shalom: House of Peace. Although the Jewish word Shalom has a much broader and deeper meaning than simply peace.

The other thing that had happened while we had been closed was that the government had brought in new laws specifically related to organizations like ours who housed people in need. The government called it "Care in the Community." After working through how this affected us and how it affected so many of the people it was meant to help, I came to the conclusion that it was a wonderful name for a government policy but there was one thing wrong with it. There was very little community, and few people really cared. I believe it was a cost-cutting measure by the government. The amount of paperwork it created was enormous. Eventually I had one staff member utilizing most of her time just on the paperwork associated with these new guidelines.

It was through this time that I started to find myself dealing more and more with government and council officers. Under these proposed new regulations relating to places such as Beth Shalom, the government had simply reworded the regulations relating to housing people in aged care facilities. I doubt whether any of the authors of these regulations had spoken to anyone running a drug rehab. The proposal was that each resident should be given a certain amount of space in their own room, with a key to their door and a lockable cupboard as well. Any speck of knowledge about drug users would have shown these people that this was not acceptable in a drug rehab. Thus, began my introduction to working with the government. Thankfully, our local MP was incredibly helpful to us through this process and we were able to adjust the regulations to suit the regime at Beth Shalom.

Chapter 20
Wandsworth prison

Apart from our work at Beth Shalom, I was also involved in other aspects of ministry as well. Our relationship with our church in Battersea had continued to grow and my own relationship with Pastor Tony was such that I saw this man as a real brother. Maybe the fact that he allowed me to preach sometimes at the church helped that? One of the ministries of the church was to send a team into Wandsworth Prison once every month. You may be aware that Wandsworth Prison was the prison that the great train robber, Ronnie Biggs, had escaped from. It was, and I believe still is, a large bluestone Victorian building right in the middle of a fashionable part of London and literally just down the road from Beth Shalom. Tony had a very good relationship with one of the chaplains at the prison and so our team would head to the prison every month and run a service for the prisoners who attended. Tony was such a natural for this work. His inbuilt pastoral giftings shone in this space. The guys who attended our services loved Tony. We would sing a few hymns, chosen by the prisoners, one of the team, Jenny, would sing and others of us would be given time to share some thoughts about life, or how faith worked. At times we would break into small groups to talk in more depth about these things. I loved being part of this team. Such a wonderful opportunity to bring a message of hope to men in a dark place. As with so many of the men I have worked with in the prisons or courts of the UK and Australia, I have found many of them to be in that situation due to what can only be described as "stupid mistakes". Not that they were innocent necessarily, but so much about their lives had led them to that place. Working with people who are caught up in the legal system is not as black and white as many people think. At the end of the day, they are real people who need Christ to show them how to change their thinking, which leads to a change of behavior. In Romans, chapter 12, the apostle Paul instructs us to be *"transformed by the renewing of your minds"*. He knew that changing the thinking would lead to a change of behavior.

Working in the prison system comes with the territory of working in the addiction field. In most cases, not all addicts have committed crime to continue their habit. The consequences of these acts are often that they end up in custody. I could say much about the subject of addictions and the legal system but that is not the purpose of this book. One thing I will say however has to do with the concept proposed by some people that addicts can be rehabilitated while inside a prison. There may be a few rare cases where this has occurred, but they would be few indeed. Prison is, by its nature, a consequence of a person's actions. They have been found guilty of breaking the laws of the land and the consequence is a term of imprisonment. A rehabilitation facility is usually a place where a person chooses to place themselves with an aim of changing their lives. A prison is a place where people are placed against their will. The staff of a prison are not there to try to rehabilitate anyone. There may be a few drug counselors on staff, but the environment works against them achieving much. Having been a drug counselor in two high security prisons in Australia I can testify to that. A rehabilitation facility is a very different environment designed to work with a person through various issues in their lives. When I hear politicians, and others, talk about their belief that people can be rehabilitated in a prison system, what I hear is a person who has little, or no, understanding of addictions at all.

One thing we needed in the new place was staff. We could not run this on our own. We had seen too many people go down that

Chapter 20 Wandsworth prison

road and burn out. Working with needy people is an emotional rollercoaster and will drain your energy very quickly. People working in these places need to make sure that they have good support networks and programs in place. Over the years in YWAM, we had seen people begin a work like ours, work at it for a few years, then go on furlough and never come back. Then someone else would take up the leadership and do exactly the same thing. June and I had decided that we needed to break that cycle. Choosing the right staff was the first step in that process. There were three things in particular that we needed in our staff. We needed someone with leadership ability. We needed someone who could lead times of worship in the house, and we needed someone who understood and could handle administration.

God provided exactly for these situations. A wonderful South African couple, Stoney and Bridget. Stony was a big South African who carried authority and could lead worship and had a great sense of humor. Bridget was gifted in administration. We thank God for this couple. Saints and Angels.

The second thing that was needed to break the cycle was a staff schedule that understood the pressures of working in a rehab. In most places of employment in a place like Britain, an employee is given three weeks annual leave as part of their employment package. There was no way that this would work in Beth Shalom. With most of the staff living on site, the pressure is always just outside your door. We eventually came up with a system that gave staff a long weekend every six weeks. A full week's leave every three months and three weeks of leave every year. On top of this, we asked staff to find an outside focus. This needed to be something that took their concentration away from the work at Beth Shalom. They could do a course at a college. They could get involved in some activity in the neighborhood, or in the case of one couple, they organized an outreach trip to somewhere in Europe. All of this was to help them see that their emotional life needed another focus. It is so easy to become so focused on the needs of the people we are working with that we forget the needs of our family, or ourselves.

So, who were these people who came to stay at the Chase and later Beth Shalom? To help the reader gain a better understanding of our work I will talk about just a couple of our residents.

Davey was one of the saddest cases I have ever dealt with. He was only about 16 when he came to us. A YWAM team had met him in the west end area of London. He had been selling himself in the pinball parlors, a stone's throw from Leicester Sq. This was a well-known haunt for pedophiles and others who abuse young people. Davey was one of five children in his family. When he was eight years old, his parents separated. His mother took two children with her and his father took two children with him, but neither of them could manage to take Davey. So, he was put into "care". Davey was in "care" for some years and always expected that one of his parents would come and bring him home. At 14 years of age, he received word that his father was coming to see him. Everything inside Davey expected that this was his dream coming true. The moment he had thought about for so long was arriving. In his mind, Dad was coming to take him home to the family. His dad arrived at the center where Davey was staying but at first his dad did not even recognize his son. When he finally realized which one of the young people in the home was his son, he then proceeded to tell Davey that his mum and he had got back together. This knowledge only served to reinforce the belief that the dream was about to come true. That, after all these years, everything would be perfect again in Davey's life. But the next part of the conversation smashed this dream to pieces. His dad informed Davey that they did not have the space to take him back with them, but they would visit at times. Just ponder that situation for a few moments and try to imagine how this young boy of 14 years of age felt at this moment.

We now know that the years in a child's life when they are going through puberty is one of the most important times for the relationship between parent and child. It is through this period that a child needs to hear words of affirmation and encouragement from

Chapter 20 Wandsworth prison

their parents. The father's role particularly during this time cannot be overestimated. At this critical time in Davey's life his parents chose to be absent.

Davey ran away from the place where he was staying and ended up in London, looking for someone to love him. Davey stayed with us for some months until one day I found him packing his bag. I asked what was going on. He then informed me that every year while he was in care someone would take him to a place called Alton Towers. A large amusement park in the north of England. He told me that it was now that time of year and he was going there and after that he was going to visit his parents to see if they would take him back again. This was a painful conversation to have with him. I tried to explain to him that he was trying to live a dream. That he had not heard from his parents for months and he was setting himself up for further pain. But the drive for parental love was so strong in this young man that he went anyway. That was the last we ever saw of Davey. Can you imagine the pain in this boy's life? The drive to be accepted into his family. The constant sense of rejection. When I think back to Davey, I just hope that something of what he heard at the Chase stuck in his soul somewhere.

Derek was another young, lost soul in London. He had come from Yorkshire and was as opinionated and stubborn as people from Yorkshire are reputed to be. I say that having grown up with a grandmother who hailed from Yorkshire.

Derek had issues around drug use, but bigger issues to do with communication. He would say whatever he wanted to whomever he wanted. The crunch came when we had a new resident move in. This young man happened to be from a West Indian background. Derek took umbrage that we would have a black person in the house, and he was quite happy to let the new guy know his feelings. This was the last straw for us, and we could not allow that sort of thing to continue. We had to ask Derek to leave. He had only been with us a few months.

AN ADVENTURE LIKE NO OTHER | *Warwick Murphy*

June and I have different recollections of how our next meeting with Derek came about, but the details of the conversation are still the same. It had been months since we had seen him and often wondered what had become of him. We accidentally came across him somewhere in London. Derek was very keen to catch up and let us know that his life had changed dramatically. He now had a job. He was in a relationship and he was active in a church in London. He wanted us to know that he had actually been listening to much of what we had said while he had been living with us and those things had brought change to his life. He was very grateful and excited to let us know.

As word spread about the work we were doing, we found that several other agencies would contact us with possible referrals who they thought might fit with what we were doing. As a result of such a referral a young lad arrived at our door one afternoon, hoping that we would accept him into our program. When I opened the door to Bradley the stench was overwhelming. He was 14 years old, standing on the doorstep in clothes that looked like he had found them in a charity bin somewhere. His shoes were too big for him and his hair had not seen a comb for quite a while. Before we could even think about interviewing him, June had taken him upstairs to the bathroom. She told him to get himself undressed, throw his clothes out the door, and get himself washed and cleaned. While he was in the bath we threw his clothes into the bin and found another outfit that would serve as his until we could organize to get him some new clothes.

I would like to say that every person who came through the Chase/Beth Shalom was a success, but that is not how these places work. Now we know that for many addicts it can take four to five attempts at recovery before they make the breakthrough. Relapse is a part of recovery. We were also on a steep learning curve ourselves and made numerous mistakes. One resident who came was another young man called Dave. The team leader from the Earls Court team called me one day and said he had been working with a guy for

Chapter 20 Wandsworth prison

some time and felt that he was now ready to go into rehab. We had a spare bed at the time, so we arranged for Richard to bring Dave around that evening. At the appointed time, the doorbell rang and I opened the door to find Richard standing there looking very apologetic, and standing next to him, or should I say barely standing next to him, was Dave. Dave had used just before Richard had picked him up and, by the time they arrived at our place, Dave was well under the influence of heroin. I learned later that this was not uncommon. Addicts going into rehab will often have one last hit.

We decided to take Dave in anyway. Dave was a similar age to myself and he became someone I got too attached to. We got on well and Dave was, for most of the time, no trouble in the house at all. As the months passed, I thought Dave was responding well to the program. However, eventually some of the other staff pulled me aside and tried to convince me that Dave was not changing at all. They were very clearly telling me that I was way too close to this guy and was not seeing the reality of his life. I disagreed at that time but eventually I had to admit that I was wrong. The truth was that Dave had not changed at all. He was still a nice guy, but he still lived in a bit of a fantasy world. To cut the long story short the last time I saw Dave he was in the exact same street where my friend, Richard, had found him that first night he arrived at the Chase. He was still using.

We continued to track with former residents for some years after their stay. Sadly, some relapsed. It is sad to hear that people you have invested so much of yourself into submit again to the old life. In two cases that come to mind, not only did their relapse affect them, but the lives of others as well. In both cases, these friends of ours had been married and had children. For several reasons both of these marriages fell apart with the subsequent effects on the wives and children. To add further pain to one story, the young friend committed suicide. These are the sides of addiction that most people never see. For the people who work in this field, it is a life of high hopes and excitement over the lives that have made it, and a life of pain and sad memories that we will carry for the rest of our lives.

Each of the residents had a story. One was a former active member of the IRA and knew that the Irish police would like to speak with him. One was a Nigerian who had overstayed his visa. They all had their own story. Most were in many ways "lost" people. For most of them, I believe that a lack of a good father was a major factor in their situation. The role of a father, during the years of puberty particularly, cannot be underestimated. This is a time when children are questioning so many things. This is a time when they need to hear words of encouragement from their father, telling them that they are the best thing since sliced bread. Sadly, the residents of Beth Shalom did not have this opportunity. The situation was that their fathers had either deserted them or were simply abusive. Possibly reproducing the actions of their own fathers.

As I sit here thinking through the list of names of those who passed through those doors, I find my heart being warmed at the memory of these people and wondering where they may be today.

Because we were a Christian rehabilitation center it was often assumed that our first priority was to "convert" these young men to Christianity. However, this was not the case. Preaching has a place and I have preached in many places from the streets to various churches, but the best preaching we could do at the Chase was to live our lives in transparency and hope that these young men would see, and be drawn to, something different. Our program was very upfront about our faith and we would talk quite openly to the residents about faith. We believe that when Christianity is explained properly it is indeed a very logical way of life, and if anyone is trying to change their life to a better one, then Christianity is well worth looking at. Our residents knew that as a team we prayed for them regularly and they knew that they could ask for prayer at any time.

There is a price to pay for being so closely involved in the lives of troubled people. As much as we had tried to build into the program ways for the staff to take care of themselves, the facts are that the longer you work so closely with people in this field the higher

Chapter 20 Wandsworth prison

the possibility of burn out. Like most issues to do with our health, particularly our mental health, these things do not just jump out at you. They come slowly and are unseen.

In my case this was certainly true. By 1994, I was physically tired and emotionally drained. The one warning sign I had noticed was that I was becoming short tempered with the behavior of some of the residents. I was vaguely aware that this was not a good thing, but I was not aware that my emotional tank was empty. Looking back from this distance, I can see that I had been operating on my own ability for some time. It is interesting to note that the more adept we become at something the more prone we are to relying on our own abilities instead of relying on God. That was where I was at.

Coupled with this was the sense that our time in the UK was coming to an end. Was it time to move on to Australia? June and I felt that this was where God was now leading us. However, my handling of the ending of our time at Beth Shalom was impacted by my lack of inner resources and if I had the time over again I would have dealt with this step quite differently. Thankfully, the running of Beth Shalom was able to be handed over to another couple who had been running a similar center in Clapham Junction, just down the road.

Looking back now, I can see that we had learned much during our time at Beth Shalom. Much about ourselves, much about working with others, and much about addictions. Those years set us up for where God has taken us since, and certainly with what we are doing today.

June and I and the children focused on making the move back to Australia. By now our eldest child was 16. Our children had basically lived their whole life in Britain. Their friends were there. Everything they knew was there. For them, this may have seemed like an adventure in some ways, but in other ways it was a wrenching, emotional time as well. June and I understood that the only life our children really knew was in Britain and leaving there would be a tough time for them. Our eldest was telling us that she did not want to move to Australia. She could move in with one of her friends from school. As we prayed, we felt that it was important for us to make the move as a whole family. If anyone felt later that they wanted to move back to Britain, then they could make that decision from Australia, but we needed to move as a whole family. Interestingly, three of our children have at times gone back to live in Britain for a time. One of them is still living there today.

June and I were of the opinion that in the sense of being led by God we were not going back; we were going forward to the next thing God had for us. This understanding of ending one thing and moving on to the next thing is important. For us we made sure that the church we had been attending, The Mish, prayed over us to see this phase in our life as ending and God sending us forward to the next thing. There should be no "going back" in the Kingdom. Only moving forward.

We were sad to leave so many good friends in London but were also excited about the future. We really had no idea what the immediate future really held. I think if we had we would not have been so excited.

PHASE 2

An Adventure is about learning.

Chapter 21

Focus on Family

When we arrived back in Australia, we were housed at the YWAM base in Melbourne for the first few months. It was a nice situation, and we are very thankful for Paul and Penny Wilcox who were living in the unit next door to us. They made us very welcome and were of great assistance as returning to Australia was more difficult than we expected. We had assumed that coming back to Australia meant that we would be working with YWAM there. But as time went on it became clear that this was not going to be the case. There really was nothing for us to get our teeth into. In our first six months in Melbourne we lived in five different houses. We had to get our children into schools. We needed a vehicle. We needed an income. We needed many things. The truth was that we felt lost. We believed that God had led us to Australia but that was about all we knew. I had an expectation that doors would open to a new role, but nothing did. We felt like we had walked into a desert in many ways, yet it is in the desert where God does a lot of His teaching. When everything is stripped away from us, we are brought back to a place of humility and in humility we can learn much. This was a place that I do not want to go to again. June and I, plus each of the children, were trying to work out where we could fit in this new place. The pastor of our church suggested that we attend a "re-entry seminar" for returning missionaries. This was a seminar to assist people, returning from service in another country, to find their feet in their new environment. The two ladies who ran the seminar were wonderful. It was here that we learned that we were now in what they called "the valley of survival". Not just June and I, but each of the children as well.

The facilitators of the seminar drew two circles. The first circle had lots of arrows pointing outwards indicating that our focus in our previous role had been outward. The second circle had lots of arrows pointing inwards indicating that now our focus had become inward on our own struggles. In our situation, each of us in the family were in our own individual bubble trying to cope with our own individual struggles. The circle with the external focus was our previous situation. The circle with the internal focussed arrows was situated in a valley that we had fallen into. We were informed that we could be in this valley for some time. We would eventually climb out of the valley and find that we were now changed. Although many of our arrows would again point outwards, there would still be a number of arrows pointing inwards.

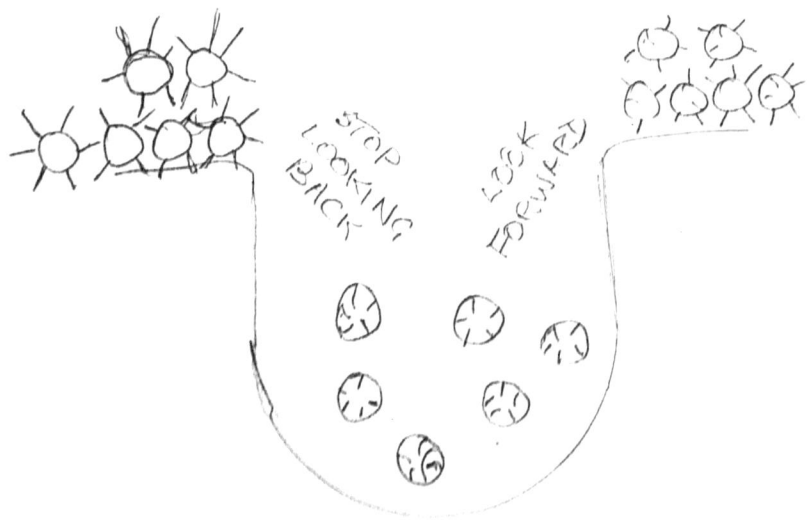

Chapter 21 Focus on Family

In Britain, we had a role, a purpose. I was heading up a residential rehab. I was on the London YWAM leadership team. I was being asked to preach in various places. We had good friends around us that we interacted with. The kids all had things they were involved with at school and church. In Australia there was none of that. Each of us in the family were in the same situation. The kids were at a new school trying to make new friends in a new culture. Yes, Australia does have a different culture to Britain. And yes, my English friends, we really do have a culture in Australia. They were in a similar situation at church, trying to find a place where they could find where they would fit. Trying to break into already established relationships. We were all trying to cope with our own individual struggles while still trying to be a family. This was one of the worst periods of our lives I have to say. I had to be honest with myself and realize that so much of my self-worth was built on my role and what I did or was seen to be doing. That may be OK for the unbeliever, but for a Christian we make the claim that we have died to ourselves and live to Christ. In my case everything had been stripped away and I was found wanting. I had to refocus and start to learn again that my identity is in Christ, not in what I do or what I can achieve. Not in what I have or how much money I can earn. Tough lessons, but if I was to be honest with myself then I had to learn the lesson. Die to self and learn again to live for Him. Not a short-term lesson.

At the seminar we learned that this situation could last from anywhere from six months to six years. Wow. Something else that we did not want to hear. I was also still unaware of how emotionally empty I was from the years of working in London. As much as I had loved the work there and had learned so much, it had drained me totally. Eventually, through a contact that our pastor connected me to, I found a job as a project officer with a group called Drug-Arm (Drug Awareness and Relief Movement). This group was the updated Temperance movement. They had a van and a team of volunteers who, each Friday and Saturday night, would drive to different parts of Melbourne and talk with many of the people living on the streets about their drug or alcohol use. They served coffee from the van and attempted to assist with referrals and other information for these people. My role was in training the volunteers and overseeing the teams as they went out.

A secondary part of my role at Drug-Arm was something new for me. Drug Arm was also a lobby group, interacting with politicians on the issues surrounding public policy on drug and alcohol use in the community. We would meet with politicians from various parties and argue our case for what laws were being introduced into Parliament, or being proposed, such as the proposition to legalize certain drugs. This part of the work is something that I have continued to be involved in ever since, albeit, in a much smaller way. The subject of government policy on drugs and alcohol in the community is an area that I keep an eye on and involve myself when I think I need to. It is possibly a subject for another book.

The timing of my step into the political world coincided with the state government putting forward proposals to decriminalize cannabis use and to open a number of heroin-injecting rooms around Melbourne. As you can imagine these proposals created uproar in the community, especially in the areas that were touted as possible places for an injecting room. The public debate went on for months and we were heavily involved in it. I found myself speaking at raucous public meetings where I shared the platform with university professors and other academics who were supporting these moves. Several organizations had come together to form a coalition opposed to what the government was proposing, and we were a part of that coalition. I had articles published in newspapers, interviews on the radio, and we were also involved in demonstrations on the steps of Parliament House in Melbourne. In short it was a loud, and at times, nasty public debate but we did see all these proposals defeated at that time.

In many ways it was nice to have a job and an income, but I still had a frustration that I was only playing on the peripheral, and

Chapter 21 Focus on Family

not assisting people in real need. So, it was time for another honest conversation with God. I think we all have these conversations at times. Conversations where we might find ourselves yelling at God, or trying to explain to Him that somehow, He has got it wrong, or is missing the point on some issue in our lives. We really do have a very limited view of the God who created all things don't we? I think that God rather enjoys these conversations because we are being very honest about things. It was in one of these conversations that I again sensed God speaking to me. It was here that He explained to me just how burned out I was when we arrived in Australia from Britain. He made me realize that the job I had with Drug-Arm was Him putting me on the back burner as it were. I was in a place where I could keep up to date with the issues to do with drugs and alcohol, but not get too involved while I recovered. It was also a job where I met many of the people in Australia who were involved in the drug and alcohol field. One of them was a Salvation Army officer I had known many years before: Major Brian Watters. Brian had been approached by the Prime Minister to act as his advisor on drug and alcohol issues. A place that I doubt Brian ever thought he would find himself in.

It was in this conversation with God that I could finally understand what He was doing with me at this stage. Finally, I could understand that I was in need of relative quiet so that I could heal. Finally, I could understand again that God's heart was always for my highest good. He does indeed know what He is doing. We just have to bend our will to acknowledge it. My time at Drug-Arm had several facets to it and overall a good time. But it was not meant to be for a long time. It had not dawned on me at the time but looking back I can see that right through this period back in Australia there was a focus on family. Our own family first, then our broader families, and thirdly the families of drug and alcohol users.

It has been said that families are the building blocks of a healthy society and we were also aware that families are God's idea in the first place. He places great importance on family. It was time for June and me to focus more on this area in our lives. Guiding our children through their teenage years with all that that entails. Finishing secondary school. Whether to go to university or not. Learning to drive. Relationships. When to loosen the reins and when to pull them back again? I know young people think it is hard going through these years, but for parents it also has tough times as well. Constantly questioning ourselves. Are we doing the right thing? When to step in to help one child deal with an issue and when to stay out of it and let them work it out themselves. When to enforce the boundaries and when to ease them off. Add into this mix that each child is different and will deal with each situation differently. For a parent these can be times of great joy and moments of heartbreak. Did we get it all right? No. I am sure that our children would have preferred we made different decisions at times, but we look at our adult children today and think we must have done something right. They are a blessing to us and many others.

One of the things I realized on returning to Australia was that I needed some recognized qualifications. In Britain, due to the work we were doing, there had not been a great call for me to gain any degrees, but in Australia I quickly realized that a qualification was a necessary item if I was going to work in this field here, or even if I was to engage people in debate about drug policy. What sort of qualification did I need though? This forced me to look at myself and start to understand that God had given me a pastoral gift. An ability to engage with people and assist them through tough times. Strangely others could see this, but I had really been blind to it. Even though the work I had done in London was all about pastoral care I had not really put a name to it. As I thought about it, I recalled an event in Amsterdam. While we had been living in Britain, we had gone to Amsterdam for a few days break as a family, and also to see the work that YWAM was doing there. Amsterdam had very soft laws around drug use and it seemed that there were dealers on every corner offering us whatever we wanted. There were, and still are, cannabis coffee shops scattered around the city and it is not hard to find whatever drug you might be after.

Chapter 21 Focus on Family

Walking through Amsterdam station one day with the family, I noticed this guy some distance away. After working with street people and users for some time we can see the signs very quickly. For these people, their history is written on their faces. Their internal pain is evidenced through the lines on their faces. This man was such a person. He looked at me and headed in my direction. He wanted to tell me all about his problems. He had picked me out from all the other people walking through that busy station. He had seen something in my face that seemed to tell him that I would listen to him. I talked with him for a short time and then turned to my family who had been waiting. One of my kids looked at me and asked if I had a sign on my forehead that said, **"People with problems please come here."** My family went on to inform me that what had just happened was not a rare event. They had seen that it was common for me to be approached by what some would call "odd people". I had never really noticed it. It is truly strange how we often think we know ourselves, but really miss the truth. How blind we can be to ourselves.

I finally opted for a Counseling Course. This seemed the obvious thing to do. I found a course that covered a wide spectrum of counseling issues and techniques. It would take a few years, but it needed to be done.

Some time after finishing the course and gaining my qualification as a Family Therapist we set up a counseling organization called "Someone Who Cares". One of my friends enjoyed telling his kids when they were complaining about something to go and call Warwick. Call Someone Who Cares (SWC).

Chapter 22

Introduction to working with families

Once again, we like to think that we are making independent decisions in our life, when often these decisions are also heavily guided by God.

This was another door opening for us. Up until this stage, working in the drug and alcohol field, we had dealt with the individual users. We had lived with them, laughed with them, and cried with them. We had learned much about many of the underlying issues that addicts need to deal with if they are to find full recovery. The behavior patterns and the deeply imbedded mindsets they have lived with. In all that time we had rarely dealt with any of the families of the addicts. Mainly because all the people we dealt with in London had either been abandoned by their families, or they had simply left home and never gone back.

Almost as soon as setting up this new counseling agency, we were introduced to families struggling with the trauma of living with an addict in their family. This was a whole new ball game. We were invited by a large church to facilitate a Family Support Group at their church. Here we heard the other side of the story. It is conservatively estimated that for every addict or alcoholic there

Chapter 22 Introduction to working with families

are at least 20 other people directly impacted by that one person. The immediate family of parents and siblings. The wider family of grandparents, aunts, uncles, and cousins. Friends and workmates. We could go on and include the police, the legal fraternity, etc.

The immediate family are living with an ongoing trauma every day. In this Family Support Group we began to hear the stories of heartache. The manipulation. The threats of violence. The lying and cheating. The divisions developed between parents who had different ideas on how to deal with the user. Story after story. Life after life. Trauma upon trauma. These were what I call the forgotten victims of the drug scene. There were plenty of services and agencies for addicts to find assistance but at that time in Melbourne there was nothing for the families.

Someone Who Cares very quickly became focused on the families. We stated that, if a family called our office, we would make sure that someone was available for them within the next 24 hours. They needed help when they called, not four or five weeks later when a space opened up on the counseling agencies program. While we were involved in counseling and supporting these people, we found that there were few churches that understood how to assist them. If a church member informs the church that they have a serious medical problem, then many people step forward and give what help they can in whatever way they can. In most cases like this we expect that there will be an end to the need at some point, that the sickness will be cured. With addictions it can seem like there is no end at all. A family can live with this for many years. Each week bringing a new problem to cope with. Many of these families slowly stop attending church or church functions. They often feel that they have failed as parents. Listening to these people, I realized something else. It seemed to me that in the church we had developed a culture of success. That on Sundays we would dress up in our nice clothes and when we met friends at church who would ask how we were, we would tell them how good life was, when, in fact, often we were struggling with all sorts of issues, both personal and relational.

I recalled a situation when we had been living in London. One Sunday morning, we had been trying to get four young children organized to get dressed and into the car for church. As often happens with children, things were not going as I would have liked, and my temper was getting thin. In the car on the way to church there was bickering in the back seat between various children and I eventually told them in no uncertain terms how they should be behaving. I was angry and fuming by the time we arrived at church. As I walked up to the front door of the church the pastor was there. He reached out his hand to greet me and said, **"How are you today, Warwick?"** I smiled nicely and said, **"Good morning. I'm fine, thanks, Tony, how are you?"** As I walked into church, the word hypocrite was very firmly on my mind.

But is not this the culture that we have developed over the years. We present to all these friends with a semi-perfect impression because we feel somehow that we might be seen as very poor Christians if we have a problem or two. When the truth is, we all have problems. We are not perfect. We struggle with the same issues that those outside the church struggle with. No, we do not need to tell everyone our troubles all the time, but we should be able to embrace those around us with non-judgmental acceptance.

Families struggling with issues of addiction feel like failures. They are embarrassed. They are hurting and they grow to feel like they are a burden in the church–they are the "problem family" in the church. They cannot tell everyone how well their child is doing at school or university. They cannot tell people that their child has a very good job. The only thing they feel they can bring to the conversation is another problem.

Slowly these families slip away, and few people notice. They may not attend church as regularly. They may not come to certain events at the church. By the time they have, in fact, stopped coming nobody notices. The church moves on.

Chapter 22 Introduction to working with families

Addictions are one of the largest problems facing every community across the globe. In fact, the issue of addiction to pornography has infiltrated the church to alarming degrees. But how many Bible Colleges have a teaching stream to do with addictions? How many pastors have taken on a church totally ill-equipped to deal with, or even understand, these bread-and-butter issues? How many youth group leaders in our churches have no idea how to deal with the drug use, the sexual identity issues, the self-harm that they are faced with each week by the youth in their care? And if you do not think that the young people in your church youth department are struggling with these issues then you need to look again. Our young people are inundated today, probably more than any other generation, with messages and information telling them how they should look, what they should believe, where to get the next adrenaline rush, and they are confused because they are not equipped to cope with it all.

Those who study these things tell us that our brains are still developing until our mid-twenties, which means that although young people think they can deal with everything, quite simply they are wrong. They need their parents and other adults to work with them through these issues. We have all heard the story about the young person who, in their mid-teens, thought their parents knew nothing about life, but by the time they were in their mid-twenties they were surprised to see how much their parents had learned in those intervening years. It may sound funny, but there is a lot of truth in that. Parents have a role to equip their children to deal with life. I would also argue that the church has a role here as well. It has been said that it takes a village to raise a child. We need to see our involvement with church as that village, but the church also needs to see its role here. In my early days in the Salvation Army in Sydney, I knew that if I stepped out of line and my parents were not around then another adult would step in and bring me into line, and I also knew that they would talk to my parents about what had occurred. So not only did I hear from that adult about my misbehavior, but I would also hear from my parents. Double jeopardy! But it is not all about the negative. There are many people from those days in my life that spoke into my life in very positive ways. Band leaders, Scout leaders. Parents of friends and so many more. These people reinforced the values of my parents at home but also showed respect to me as a person.

Through our work with these families, I was beginning to see that the church, in many ways, is ill-equipped to deal with these situations. That the church needs to re-evaluate their training methods for the good of, not only their own people, but understanding the community outside of the walls of the church building. If they are to reach out to these people, then they have to understand them first of all. God was planting a seed in my heart that would grow over the next years and bear fruit.

I loved this new side of our work. The families were always wanting to learn about addictions. What makes their family members continue on that road? How do we deal with these situations when they arise? Can we put boundaries in place where they have been torn down? These people were hungry and responsive, and it was a delight to work with so many of them. We learned so much through these families and are still in touch with several of them today. In fact, our work with families continued well after Someone Who Cares closed its doors.

I had a call one day from a lady who had attended one of the support groups that we had facilitated. She informed me that her son had been arrested again for drug related crimes. I had worked with her son for a few years and had a good relationship with him, but I was not surprised to hear that he was back in police custody again. By the time this lady called me, this young man had been moved from police cells to the assessment prison in the city. As it turned out this was a prison where I found myself working a few years later. This prison is like the prisoner-sorting house of Victoria. Every male in custody in Victoria will go through this facility. Some are held on remand while others are waiting to be transferred to another prison once they have been sentenced.

Chapter 22 Introduction to working with families

The visiting room is not unlike what we often see in the movies. Little cubicles where the prisoner is separated from the visitor by a glass wall and conversation takes place via a phone connection. After going through the normal security checks that everyone entering the prison has to go through, I was shown into one of the cubicles to wait while they brought the young man down from upstairs. He walked in, realized who his visitor was and shook his head. He sat down, picked up the phone, and said to me, *"Why do you keep coming after me?"* What a great opportunity to speak into his life about his inherent value that he carries because he is made in the image of God.

While all this was going on, God was opening another door as well. My friend in England, David Partington, had been instrumental in the formation of a networking agency for Christians working in the addiction field. David and a team of others had started a ministry called ISAAC (International Substance Abuse and Addiction Coalition). ISAAC had an office in England and David was the General Secretary of ISAAC, while still holding the reins at Yeldall Manor. David had received an email from a lady working among trafficked women in China, asking for someone to come and give them some training on how to deal with addictions, as most of the women they were working with had an addiction issue. These women had been sold into brothels in China and this woman and her team were responding to the need.

David sent out an email to all ISAAC members and when I read the email it was like it jumped off the page at me. I talked to June about it and it seemed to us that China was in our part of the world and why would we not respond? Thus began a whole new adventure which we will get to later. Suffice to say, at this stage that trips to Asia became a regular thing from then on.

As an agency working with the families, SWC was able to gain a Federal Government grant that supported our work. The Prime Minister of the day had a concern in this area and was keen that his government was involved. The grant was given on an annual basis and meant that we had to reapply each year. However, after two years we had a change of government and the grant was stopped. We had to close the door quite suddenly, although we did not suddenly cease from working with the families on our books, but I did need to find other work. Back to prayer. By now I was of the firm belief that it is God that opens doors for us. I knew that God would have something for me somewhere.

Chapter 23
Working in Prisons

A position opened for a drug counselor to work in two of the maximum-security prisons in Melbourne. I applied, had an interview and was given the position. Once again, a whole new ball game. Working in a prison means adhering to the rules probably more than most jobs, and having your background thoroughly checked out. A few days after I started, I was called in to see my supervisor. She had a list of prisoners' names in front of her and said to me, *"While we have been looking at your background, we discovered that you have some connection with these prisoners. That you have been to this prison to visit them previously. This is something of a concern to us. What is your relationship to these men?"* She was basically telling me that I might be a security problem in the prison. I started to smile as I realized the names on the list were individual addicts I had been working with over the years. I went through the list with her one-by-one detailing what I could recall of that person and trying to explain that I had visited them in prison because they were people of some value. This she did not understand. Certainly, she had no understanding of them having value. But more, she had never met another drug counselor who visited their clients in prison. I was an enigma. She finally seemed OK with things but did inform me that she would have to bring this before the prison governor, and we would have to wait to see what he would do about it. As it happened, he had some concerns but was happy to let me work on a trial basis which eventually became a full-time position.

AN ADVENTURE LIKE NO OTHER | *Warwick Murphy*

June and I have always felt that our work with the addicted was not about a client/counselor situation. We have always seen it as a friendship relationship, yet with a balance of the client/counselor situation as well. To many counselors this will sound like heresy. Counseling courses talk a lot about dual relationships. That, if a person is a client, then the counselor should not be spending time with them in any other manner. I can understand this in most counseling situations, but when it comes to addictions I find I must disagree with this concept. One of the basic needs of the addict is relationships. People addicted to drugs or alcohol have been rejected by most others. Family, society, mates, etc., and we fully understand why this is the case, but that does not mean that God rejects them, and if we are trying to be Jesus to them then we need to find a way of developing a working relationship where possible. The same can be said for other addictions, particularly the current pandemic of addiction to pornography that we see across the world today.

I quickly became aware I had a sense that I had met many of these men before. I knew the truth was that I had not met all these prisoners, but I could not shake this feeling. It finally came to me that the men I was meeting in these prisons were very similar to the men I had met in Wandsworth Prison in London all those years ago. It really is strange that people in similar situations on the other side of the globe can be similar in behavior and outlook on life. I have seen it in prisons. I have seen it in welfare offices. I have seen it on the streets. The women that often get called "bag ladies" look the same whether they are in London or Melbourne or New York. Men in a prison are also similar. Even the dumb reasons why they are in prison are similar.

This was a tough gig. Oftentimes I would have a really good conversation with a prisoner with a real sense that he was growing in his understanding of his behavior and thinking patterns, only to find that when he left the conversation and ventured back out into the prison yard he had to put on the façade that they all have. Anything he learned in the conversation was lost on the doorstep.

Chapter 23 Working in Prisons

Prison is a place of lost hope, lost dreams, and lost futures. Can people change in prison? Yes, they can. But few do. I recall a conversation with a group of prisoners one day. I asked them, *"How many of you have been in prison more than once?"* Probably 80% of the hands went up. Some of these guys had been inside five to six times. I then asked them, *"How many never want to come back again?"* 100% of the hands went up. My next question was, *"How many of you, when you do get out, will go back to the same neighborhood you came from?"* All hands in the air. *"How many of you will drink at the same pub you always drink at?"* All hands again. *"How many of you will hang out with your mates again?"* All hands in the air again. My last question was simply, *"If you are going to do all that, why do you think you will never come back here again?"* If you are not going to change anything then nothing will change. In recovery circles, people say, *"If nothing changes, nothing changes."* It has been said that the definition of insanity is doing the same thing over and over and expecting a different result. This is what these men were telling me. They wanted a different outcome in their lives. They wanted a better life, but they did not want to change anything about their lives. It just does not work that way for any of us. If we want to change the behavior, then we have to look at our lives and decide what factors need to change to gain the desired result.

Working in a prison, hoping to see change, is a very frustrating thing. Seeing the same faces appear again a few weeks after being released drains the energy out of a person.

During my time working at the prisons, I was also doing trips to Asia to run training sessions on addictions in various places. I was using up my holiday times, my sick days, and any other times I could cobble together to allow me to do these trips. Eventually, I had no more days that I could wrangle. Change was about to take place again.

PHASE 3

An adventure enlarges vision

Chapter 24
ISAAC Australasia

By 2010, our trips to Asia were a regular thing. We had started with an invitation to China for two weeks. From that initial trip invitations were coming from other places as well. We quickly found ourselves in Asia two to three times a year. I found myself not just speaking on issues to do with addictions, but being asked to speak to students at a Family Counseling School or address the issues of abuse and the treatment of women. To consider that poverty is the underlying issue in so many countries that leads to so much pain. I had to begin the long road of grappling with how much our culture impacts so much of what we do in life and how we see the world.

When people ask me where we have worked, I tell them from Mongolia to Indonesia. From Pakistan to the Philippines. Asia is a large region and there is much to do and there are many amazing people reaching out to meet the need.

I went to Asia as a representative of ISAAC International. I had a growing sense that God had more for us to do in Asia than just visit a few times a year. As usual for me it was a bit vague to start with. Each trip I met new people doing extraordinary things with very little. One lady from Korea had moved to Mongolia and had started working with alcoholics there, of which there are many. She had started working with a few people running a program called Celebrate Recovery. Now, all these years later that ministry is right across Mongolia with a wonderful team of people reaching out to other alcoholics. On that first trip, I realized that the Russians had only departed Mongolia 16 years previously. One of the things they left behind, apart from some very ugly buildings, was an enormous alcohol problem. This group set up an alcohol recovery group based on the Celebrate Recovery model, and out of those early groups they have gone on to planting churches as families respond.

I met an English lady living in Hong Kong who has become a very good friend. She has been there for 50 years. Many years previously, she felt God call her to missions, but she could not find a mission agency that would take her on. So finally, she got on a boat leaving Britain and told God that she would get off when He told her to. Each time the boat docked in a city she would ask God, "Should I get off here?" Finally, the ship stopped in Hong Kong and she felt this was where she was to get off. She had no Chinese language. No contacts and very little money. Now, 50 years later, she heads up one of the most amazing ministries I have ever seen. Beginning with a large work among the addicted in Hong Kong and going on to plant a church that is reaching out to the poverty-stricken thousands in that city. Not to mention the teams from her work that are spread out across other parts of Asia.

We have met champions of faith working in hostile territory and, while not hiding their faith, they are ministering to some of the neediest situations one could imagine. These are people who are not seeking recognition from anyone. They are simply getting on with the work that God has called them to do. I will not mention any names here as many of them are working in what can only be described as hostile territory for a Christian. Right across Asia there are hundreds of organizations doing extraordinary things.

As I related earlier, I had used up all my spare days at the prison, including holidays, to make trips to Asia. Now God brought me to a crossroads. I had an invitation to run another training session in Asia. ISAAC International had a leaders' gathering in Europe

Chapter 24 ISAAC Australasia

that they wanted me to attend and I also had an invitation to a conference in Asia. These three events were going to happen within a couple of weeks of each other. I believe God had brought me to this place. I could continue to stay in Melbourne and work at the prison, or I could resign from the prison work and step into a full-time role with ISAAC in the Asian region. One option had the benefit of an income and a sense of security, the other option had no discernible income, no discernible security, and the possibility of working among what to me were strange cultures with strange food and languages. On the surface it seemed like an easy choice. Trust God or myself. As I prayed it grew more and more obvious. I recall sitting in my little office at home and having a direct conversation with God. I told him that I would eagerly take on the role in Asia. It was to me the obvious decision. If that was what God was opening, then why do anything else? However, I also said to Him that I would take on the role, but I was not going to chase funds to make it happen. I had done this for 30 years and I was not good at it. I recalled Winkey Pratney saying to us one day, *"Make it easy on yourself and hard on God."* I explained to God, like He needed me explaining, that provision was His job, not mine. If He wanted me to take this step, and remember it was not just me, it was my family too, then He needed to raise the finances to make it happen. I have to say that at this point I could almost hear God cheering. It seemed like He was saying, *"He finally gets it. It's my job, not his."* Thus began the next step in this life of adventure with God.

After that conversation with God I recall relating it to someone. After listening to my tale, they said to me, *"So what do you think is going to happen?" Do you think someone is just going to drop money on your doorstep?"* I said I have no idea, but it is not my concern. While everything inside me was screaming just the opposite. The very next morning, as I walked out my front door, I felt something under the doormat. I bent down and picked up an envelope. Inside was $1500 in cash. I laughed out loud and immediately messaged my friend to tell Him that God did actually leave something on the doorstep. I have no idea who left that money and I have not seen that happen again. I believe that God was having a bit of a laugh though. The other thing that came out of that, I felt like God was assuring me that He could and would provide as we took this next step. June and I had determined that we would not embark on a trip unless the funds were there to do so. No putting it on a credit card. If God was going to provide then we would let Him do that. The other thing I determined was that I was not going to go around asking people for money to support us. I believe there is a place for this, and I am aware of many people who are supported in this manner. In fact, many mission organizations will not let you go overseas until you have raised a certain amount of funds to support yourself. I have no problem with this at all. God can provide in any way that He sees fit and that is between the person and God. In our case, I felt strongly that we should not be appealing for funds as a general rule. If someone wants to know about our finances, I am happy to have that conversation with them, but I will not raise it myself. If some people want to have a fundraising event for our work, I have no problem with that either. Our decision to not ask for funds is what I felt before God that we should do. I make no judgment on anyone else as to how they go about raising support.

In the past 10 years I have not asked anyone for financial assistance for our personal needs, and I do not intend to. We have included the bank details of the ministry in our newsletters, but I do not make any appeal for our personal funds. I have made appeals for funding for the ministry, but we keep our finances and the ministry finances as two separate things.

Chapter 25
First Steps in Asia

Our first steps into Asia were exciting, and at the same time, a bit unnerving. This was a whole new phase in our lives taking us into new fields and where very little was familiar. We had learned by this time that following where God leads will take us into these new places and the difference we found this time was that, although being apprehensive, we were also far more confident in God to be able to take this step with a greater degree of certainty.

We were traveling up to Asia from our home in Australia on a regular basis and it did not take long for the question to arise in our minds, *"Should we move to Asia?"* Two main reasons kept coming to mind to ask this question. One was the cost factor, and the other was the amount of time spent traveling there and back again. Surely it was smarter to just base ourselves somewhere in Asia and then take relatively short trips to the various countries from our base.

This question was at first just a thought, but one that grew over time and found us thinking more and more about making the move to base ourselves somewhere in Asia. Thinking about making such a move was somewhat easy while it was just a thought. Looking at all the surrounding issues created quite a different scenario. Most of our family were in Australia, including elderly parents. We were carrying responsibility for a degree of care for our two remaining parents, having already lost a mum, in June's case, and a father in mine. There were also other issues to do with our house, which needed to be dealt with. So, we waited. While we were waiting, we prayed, and looked at different cities in Asia where we might live. However, we did not really decide on a particular city until we were in a position to actually make such a move. Now it was time to make some firm decisions. Through this waiting time we had become convinced that relocating was what we should be doing.

One thing we did find was that through this period of waiting we were talking more and more to each other, and other friends, about actually moving to live in Asia. I realized after a time that this is one of those steps of faith that people need to take as they walk the road of faith. The Bible says in the book of Hebrews, chapter 11, that *"faith is the substance of things hoped for. **The evidence of things not seen.**"* One of my friends calls it a "confident expectation". To be talking about things that to mortal eyes cannot be seen, as though they are very real. This is probably one of those areas that people who are not believers struggle with. In fact, in truth, it is an area where a lot of believers struggle too. Is the invisible world more real than the visible? Once again, we need to go back to scripture to see that there is a realm that mortal eyes cannot see. In the Bible, the book of 2 Kings, chapter 6, we read that the prophet Elisha prayed for his servant to have his eyes opened so that he could see that, although their present situation looked very grim in the natural, God had placed a vast unseen army around them to take them to victory.

Steps of faith would not be faith if we could see only with our physical eyes. Faith means stepping out on the Word of God and trusting that God will bring to pass what He has said He will. Each of the major steps in our lives up until this stage had been steps into the seemingly unknown. This would be no different.

Eventually, things in Australia had come to a place where we were able to focus on this next step. June's father had passed away, and some time later my mum also passed into eternity. But where should

Chapter 25 First Steps in Asia

we move too? Asia is a big place. We looked at a few different places, but eventually decided that Kuala Lumpur, Malaysia, was the best option. We had several friends living there. Air Asia is based there, and they fly right across Asia at what, at times, are very cheap fares. So, that is where we finally moved to. We rented a nice little flat in a suburb of KL, in the same block as good friends who lived upstairs. These friends, Kenneth and Priscilla, and their two teenage children, were incredibly helpful in seeing us settle in and find our way around in those first days and we are eternally grateful to them and their children. Saints and Angels.

Chapter 26

Learning about culture

Asia is like nowhere else on earth. For someone who was raised in Australia it has always been a region to our north, and indeed in our geographical locality, but not a place where we have ever felt "at home". Australia's modern history when I was growing up was closely aligned to the UK due to our history. In more recent times we have seen our political and security alliances come a lot closer to the US. And yet here we are just south of Asia and yet not part of Asia. Who are we? We are a little outpost of the western world, sitting close to Asia and to the Pacific Island nations. Most of our trade these days is with Asia. Lots of people these days are taking holidays in Asia. Many of our school children are learning Asian languages, and our universities have a large percentage of Asian students enrolled in them. Our larger cities all have significant Asian populations living there. Much different from what I experienced while growing up in Sydney. Back then the only connection to Asia was the Chinese restaurant up the road. Asian and Australian cultures are totally different. In the twenty-first century, Australia is still not sure where it fits geographically. Much like the first westerners who came here in the eighteenth century we love the country but somehow, we know there is a strong umbilical cord that ties us culturally to somewhere else.

Chapter 26 Learning about culture

I recall our first trip to Asia. Talk about culture shock. Everything was different. The traffic was so crazy I was taking videos of it. The electric wiring down each street just looked like a conglomeration of wires and required more photos. The food was different. The language was different. Even the toilets were different. We must have walked around with our mouths agape. Even though I had prepared teaching notes I quickly realized that so much of my notes were not relevant to the situation I was in. There are so many stories I could relate about the differences we found and how we dealt with them. We were out of our comfort zone in a big way. Because the country we had been invited to, China, was waging a war against faith we were confronted with issues of security that we needed to adhere to. We were given a mobile phone for emergency situations. Our conversations in public had to be in a sort of code. The first place we were taken to for a teaching session was in the home of a lovely family. We were driven as close to the front door of the block of flats as they could get the van. I went to open the door and was quickly told not to do that. To wait till someone made sure it was safe and they would open the door and we were then to move quickly into the foyer of the block. Once inside, we were rushed up the stairs and into the unit. Inside were maybe 50 people crammed into a space that might be comfortable for 10 people at most. They were waiting to hear what I had to share.

Government policy at the time in China was such that any gathering of more than 10 people had to have permission from the government. This was our first taste of the underground church in China. Under the present leadership, the situation for Christians, and indeed people of any faith, is much worse. Whole communities of Muslims are taken to "re-education camps" to straighten out their thinking, to bring it into line with Communist Party thought. Thousands of people are sentenced to years in prison simply because they claim faith in Christ. People are tortured and others just disappear. Children of Christian parents are denied a place at school. They have even come to the decision to rewrite the Bible so that it conforms to Party policy. This is the history of Communism throughout the world. They will not broach anyone having thoughts of their own that differ to the party. George Orwell did not know how prophetic he was.

The interesting thing though is that Christianity has bloomed in China through all this opposition. The church has grown like nowhere else in the world. On subsequent trips to China we have met some amazing people who are willing to risk their freedom, and in many cases their very lives, to share the message of the God who loves them to many, many people. These are not high-flying pastors being feted by many. These are men and women who are basically peasants who have been raised from the gutter and reborn as leaders. They have no wage and, in many cases, they have no home. They travel from village to village teaching the faith that has changed their lives. They risk imprisonment every day and yet they deem it of no importance so that others can hear the message of freedom that changed their lives.

The teaching sessions I had prepared had been all about addictions and although many in the group were keen to learn as they were working in that field, to others it meant little. I realized that, even though we had gone there to teach on addictions, there was also an expectation that we would bring another message. These people wanted teaching from the scriptures. They wanted to learn more about God and His ways. They were the hungriest Christians I had ever met. I was happy to broaden the subjects that I was talking about but this then opened up another unexpected situation. On this first trip, and subsequent trips I was confronted with a clash of culture. Not between my culture and theirs, but between their culture and the culture of the Kingdom of God.

In the city of China that we were in as part of the teaching that I was doing on addictions, I was talking about the fact that a common factor with addictions is that the person will tell lies. Not just one or two, but constant lies. They lie by choice and they lie by omission. By not telling the whole story about something. They lie about what drugs they are using, and how much of that drug they are using. Lying is just a fact of life with anyone with an addiction problem. It is often said in recovery circles. How can you tell when an addict is lying? When their lips are moving. As I talked about this to the group I was teaching, I related that, if we are living a life as a Christian, we should not be lying. If we are talking to the people we are working with and asking them to stop lying then we must make sure that we are living a life of truth as well, just as we are called to do in the Bible. One of the young staff members raised his hand and said, **"Are you trying to tell us that we should not lie?"** I said it is not me telling you this, it is the Bible. It is very clear. He then said to me, **"But everyone in this city lies, that's part of who we are."** I was thrown by this. I must have looked like it as the leader of this organization said to me that the people in this city were known for their lying. They have been like that for centuries and see it as part of their way of life. I was not just presenting a biblical concept; I was challenging their culture without even being aware of it. Other incidents occurred over the next year or two that pushed me to begin thinking about how deeply embedded culture is in our lives. I was being brought to a place of seeing that there are deep roots in all our lives that are in a battle with what Jesus talked about when He talked about the Kingdom of God.

Other examples that I was confronted with, and I use that word purposefully because these things were very much in my face, pushed me further down this stream of thought.

One of the things I had noticed in China, and in many parts of Asia, was that women seemed to be treated as second class people. Not just by governments, but by the men in their lives as well. In this same city, I had been asked to talk about the value of women. That they are not lesser people. That in God's eyes they are of the same value as any man. I began by asking the group how many people thought women were treated well in China. To my great surprise all the hands in the room went in the air. I was shocked. I then spent the rest of the teaching that day talking about the value of women and trying to give a biblical view on this subject.

The next morning as the group was gathering, I noticed that one woman had rushed in and was telling anyone who wanted to listen about something that had happened to her on her way to the meeting. I did not want to miss out on her story so I asked someone to explain. As this lady was making her way to the session that morning, she had taken her young son to a shoe store to get him some new shoes. She related how she went into the shop and asked to see some shoes for her son. The assistant brought one pair of shoes for her to look at. The lady then asked if they had other shoes that she could see. The shop assistant took great offence at this and after an angry discussion he threw her out of his shop and told her not to come back. She was understandably quite upset. However, I realized that here was a great example of what I had been trying to get them to see. So, I asked the group would the same thing have happened if the boy's father had taken him into the shop? The room burst into laughter at my question. So, I had to ask again for an explanation, to be told that it was not a man's job to get shoes for his children. It is the woman's role. After we all settled down, I asked the group to consider the question anyway. If the father had taken his child into the shop would he have been treated in the same manner? Would he have been thrown out? Not at all they told me. There may have been strong words, but he would never have been thrown out of the store. So, I then asked the group, if women can be treated in such a way in China, why do you think that they are well treated? Some of them started to understand what I was saying, but I realized that their culture was so embedded in their lives that they could not immediately see any problem with the treatment of women.

This pushed me to consider my own culture. How deeply in my life are things embedded that seem so normal? What things reside in my life that I am blind to? What areas of my life and culture are at odds with the culture of the Kingdom of God?

On another trip to Mongolia, I had also been asked to speak on the issue of the value of women, particularly on the issue of domestic

Chapter 26 Learning about culture

violence. It is a long standing, deep-seated problem in that country. I spent a day laying a groundwork of how God sees women. Of how He values women. The next morning, I began to narrow the subject down to the issue of abuse that females in Mongolia have to live with. After speaking on this issue for some time I was surprised when a lady in the group raised her hand and said, *"But that is how we do things here in Mongolia."* She was one of those being abused and yet here she was defending the abuse because it was just a cultural issue to her, and I was an outsider who just did not understand. She was not hearing a message about Kingdom values. She was only hearing an ignorant westerner interfering where he should not be.

Chapter 27
What is Kingdom Culture?

These situations caused me to look again at Jesus' teaching about the Kingdom. The Bible says that Jesus came, preaching the Kingdom of God. He did not come preaching John 3:16. His Gospel, His good news, was about the Kingdom of God. He said to people, *"The Kingdom is among you."* As I went back to the scriptures, I could see that He spoke a lot about the Kingdom and His actions spoke loudly of something different to the culture He was living in. He was, in fact, confronting the culture of the day that the Pharisees and other leaders had developed and exhibiting a whole new way of living. His attitude toward women was almost entirely confrontational to that culture. His attitude toward finances was at odds with that culture. The more I looked at the way He lived and taught the more I came to see that, in many ways, culture can, in fact, imprison us and conform us to certain behavior patterns and ways of thinking that are just at odds with Kingdom culture. Surely, if Jesus spoke so much about the Kingdom of God, then we have a need to try to understand what that is. If Jesus is introducing us to this Kingdom then where have we been living up till now, and what are the differences between the kingdom we have been living in and the Kingdom that Jesus talked about?

Chapter 27 What is Kingdom Culture?

So here I was thinking we had come to Asia to "bring" something of change to issues on addiction in this region and God was showing me that it was Him who was changing the way I see the world. When we find ourselves in strange places the temptation is to try to change that situation when, in fact, it is we who need to adapt to the situation. This study has shown me that we have a choice whether we continue to live in the kingdom we have been raised in, or we can choose to live in the Kingdom that Jesus brought. I also realized that much of our work in Asia is the result of all the training that God had taken us through in earlier years. I believe that we have a measure of expertise in our knowledge of addictions, particularly drug and alcohol addiction, and we also have a degree of knowledge of how God works in certain areas. All of this was now bearing fruit in what we were called to do in Asia. The lessons of dependence on God for finances, housing, employment, and so much more, that we had been learning over the years were now bearing fruit. The lessons on God's character and how He governs were bearing fruit. It was as though so much of our lives had been preparing us for such a time as this.

Were we the only ISAAC people doing anything in Asia? Not at all. ISAAC is a network of organizations. It is not a top-down organization. We have other people who have been in the region much longer than us who are also working here although for the most part their main role is working with another organization first, and their focus on the ISAAC role is secondary.

What did we hope to do in Asia?

I quickly realized that throughout Asia there are many, many small non-government organizations (NGOs) operating in hostile environments. It may be as I have described in China, a Communist regime antagonistic to the message of Christianity. It may be a nation based on another faith, such as Islam or Buddhism or Hinduism.

These people I met were fulfilling a call on their lives to bring the Gospel to the people in their nation. To do this they need to be wise. To some degree they keep their head down and just get on with their work.

In the west, we have had the privilege of being able to be very open about our faith, although that is now changing in some western countries. We can find it relatively easy to raise funds and interact with the government. In Asia that is not the case. I realized that in Australia, as a person working in the addiction field, I could attend numerous training courses at numerous colleges. I could attend seminars almost every month if I wanted. In short, I had access to information and methods that my friends in Asia could not. One thing I was seeing in some parts of Asia was a process where a person might come through a rehab to recovery, then stay on in the rehab as a staff person, and in some cases then going on to open another rehab reproducing the only method of recovery they had ever known.

In one country, a young lady who had gone through a government rehab program explained to me that in that program she had been chained to a bed while she went through withdrawal. Interestingly, it was in that government rehab facility that she became a believer. When I met her, she was setting up a rehab in the hills outside of that country's capital city. While we were driving up there one morning, she asked me if I thought it would be OK to chain their new residents to the bed while they went through withdrawal, or was there another way? Needless to say, we then had a long conversation about some other options that could be used, and this conversation was overlaid with the more important factor of respecting the people we are working with.

On a recent visit to the north of Thailand, in fact right on the border with Myanmar, I had a conversation with my translator, a young man from Myanmar. I had been teaching a group of Bible school students about addiction, for some days. This young man

Chapter 27 What is Kingdom Culture?

implored me to come back again the following year. He said he wanted me to talk to pastors in Myanmar about addiction as he saw that the church could contribute to the response to the massive addiction problem in that country. He explained to me that just 20 kilometres from where we were talking there was a Burmese government rehab facility housing over 200 addicts. These people were all chained to their beds through withdrawal and then chained to another addict through the rest of their 12 months stay in that place. They were periodically beaten to teach them that drug use was a bad thing.

In other parts of Myanmar, we have seen videos of camps where workers in the Jade mines of Myanmar live. These people are often paid for their labor with heroin. The drug is so cheap in this part of the world that the criminals who run these mines think it is better to pay people with heroin rather than actual money.

On one trip to northern Thailand I stood where three countries meet. Thailand, Myanmar, and Laos. This is known as the Golden Triangle. This place is notorious for the trafficking of heroin through the region and on to the outside world. The locals are so proud of this fact that I was shown into one of the local highlights for tourists. The Heroin Museum, highlighting the history of this trade.

Addiction is a very complex issue but one of the main drivers of addiction in Asia is poverty. So many people are exploited by unscrupulous criminals that they see it is better to get high on heroin than have to face the reality of their poverty each day.

God was opening up ways for us to bring a different message. A message of love and respect for broken people. A message of hope for the future. A message that says, *"You are important, and you don't need to live like this."*

In my 40-odd years of working in the addiction field I have learned that there are many methods of recovery from addiction, but there is not one method that fits all. I have seen someone leave one rehab because they could not make it work and go on to another place with a different program that works for them.

I did not want to see any rehab change their method, but I did want to see them understand that there are other methods that work, and there are things they can learn from some of these other methods. You could liken it to a mechanic having a toolbox. In his toolbox he has a variety of spanners and screwdrivers. He has a variety of different tools for the different situations that he might be confronted with when he looks under the hood of the next car that comes into his workshop.

For the person working in the addiction field, it can be similar. But if you only have one tool in the box then you are very limited as to what you can realistically achieve. God has made every person different. Two people will respond to the same situation quite differently. As counselors, we need to have a toolbox with a variety of tools (methods) so that we can adapt to the way the next person in our work is trying to handle a situation.

We started working in Asia by bringing some teaching on addictions to the various groups that invited us. The teaching on addictions branched out to include Bible teaching, naturally. We do not just want to see people stop using drugs, we want to see them change their whole lives for the better. Simply stopping the drug use is relatively easy. Changing the mindset that drives the addiction is another thing entirely. If it is simply a behavioral change then it can only continue if the person constantly makes the hard choice to stop and if they are faced with a crisis in their life during this time, then the chances are that they will relapse and go back to using again. If they really want to see permanent change, then they must change their thinking. This is not just a Christian concept. Any rehabilitation program worth their salt will go down this road. The 12-step programs that operate all over the world such as Alcoholics Anonymous or Narcotics Anonymous are

Chapter 27 What is Kingdom Culture?

based on people changing their thinking. When you think about it, if you have tried to change some form of behavior in your life, such as trying to lose some weight, or to stop smoking, you will have had to alter your thinking to come out as successful on the other side.

Of course, Christianity is all about change. In the book of Romans, chapter 12, verses 1 and 2, we read, ***"Be transformed through the renewing of your mind that you may know what is the will of God."*** This is the apostle Paul teaching us this basic thing, and he knew something about having to change his thinking if anyone did.

As an addict changes their thinking, they gradually see their whole lives change.

So, the addition of Bible teaching was a natural progress for us.

The second factor that kept happening was related to the issue of pastoral care. I found that the leaders of the places I visited were often struggling with personal issues in their own lives. If I was visiting a particular organization it was not a rare thing to have one of the leaders want to get some one-on-one time with me to talk through issues that they had no one else to go to about. When I go to China, the lady who runs the work there always says to me, ***"I need a whole day with you to discuss a number of things."*** So we will find a local tea or coffee shop and sit there while she offloads, and I can hopefully bring some input that may assist her to deal with some of those issues that she has raised. She keeps inviting us back there, so our input must be helpful. This side of the work I was not expecting, but I found I was enjoying it. The pastoral gifting that God had placed inside me, plus the counseling training was all being put to good use. The lessons we had learned over the years were all bearing fruit in our lives and the lives of others now. Although in many ways we may have found the lessons tough at the time we were now enjoying the fruit of those lessons.

AN ADVENTURE LIKE NO OTHER | *Warwick Murphy*

I may have been doing the teaching, but my wife was also doing her part. June has a great interest in craftwork, and she always took some of this with her on a trip. She sat in the teaching sessions doing some of this work, and during the breaks in teaching many of the women gathered round her to see what she was doing. This opened many opportunities for deeper conversations with these ladies. It is not always the person up at the front doing the obvious thing. God often works through those people working quietly in the background.

June impacts people wherever she goes. People enjoy interacting with her and listening to her stories of events that we have lived through. In fact, I believe that most of these people remember June far more than they remember me at times. I find that if I arrive at a meeting or conference without her the first question I hear from people is, **"Where's June?"** They are disappointed if she is not with me. Never underestimate the impact that you might have on someone else.

The third thing that we are involved with is the facilitating of an ISAAC Asia Regional Conference every two to three years. ISAAC International had been running international conferences for some time. The first one being in Canterbury, England, in 1999, followed by others in Spain and Egypt. People literally came from all over the world to these conferences. We did see that for many people from the Asian region attendances at one of these conferences was a problem. A problem of time and cost, and at times of not being able to get a visa. So, as a few of us talked, we realized we could run a regional conference that hopefully would make it a lot easier for our friends in the region to attend. We also thought it would be helpful if we could move the conference around the region. To that end we have now run conferences in Kuala Lumpur, Malaysia; Phnom Penh, Cambodia; Yangon, Myanmar; and Kathmandu, Nepal. Attendance can be in the region of 150 to 200 people, and they get to meet others in the region doing similar work. They are exposed to teaching and workshops on a variety of subjects, and the interaction between sessions and over meals is incredibly stimulating.

Chapter 27 What is Kingdom Culture?

These conferences can also have other unexpected benefits. The conference in Myanmar gave the local ISAAC members a profile that they had not had before. At our conferences where the locals feel it is appropriate, we will invite to the opening session some local dignitaries. People such as government ministers and leaders of the various faiths in that country. In Myanmar, we saw two government ministers attend the opening session along with a leader from the Buddhist faith. The government ministers recognized that this conference was facilitated by an international organization and had drawn people from across the globe. This gave some prestige to the local workers which opened doors after the conference. We have not been able to do that in every conference, but we will continue to make those invitations where possible.

While I write this, we are in the middle of the Covid-19 pandemic that has closed down so much of the world. We are sitting in our unit in Kuala Lumpur with limited options for movement in our area, much like the rest of the world. This has limited the face-to-face interaction with our friends in the region and we have had to look at new ways to deal with that. Emails and video messages have been helpful, as well as assisting financially where possible as several of our friends are involved in providing food packages to people in their neighborhoods who do not have access to the basics for living. God has not forgotten these people and His church is reaching out.

Chapter 28

Still on the Road

How long will we be here in Asia? We are not sure. The day will come when it will be time to step back and let others take over. We will do as we have always done, and that is to follow the leading of our wonderful God. At this stage, we still have the energy and desire to keep reaching out and will continue to make ourselves available to God and to our friends in Asia.

Now, after 45 years of working with broken people, I look back down the road that we have been on and stand amazed at what God has done. From that confused young man in Sydney, Australia, trying to live a life in two camps, to where we are today is nothing short of a miracle in itself. The adventure that I had dreamed of back then was simply a self-centered dream that was designed to make me feel good and feed the innate selfishness that was resident in my heart.

I have learned so much about God and His ways. I have learned so much about myself that I never knew. God has wrought change in this broken life so that I might try to bring change to other broken lives. I have come to love these broken people so much. In fact, these days I do not see them as broken people. I see people with gifts that they have not discovered yet. People with as much potential as anyone else. People who can go on to reach out to others. I see people of substance and hope. I believe that when God looks at us, He does not see the same thing that we see when we

Chapter 28 Still on the Road

look in the mirror. We see the negatives in our lives. He sees the person He created us to be. He sees the gifts and abilities that He has placed in all of us. All different gifts but designed to work together with others, in humility.

In the counseling room I have often asked clients to write out a list of the 10 things they do not like about themselves and another list of the 10 things they do like about themselves. In every case, the person will tell me how easy it was to do the first list and how hard it was to do the second. Often, they could not complete the second list. This is because we believe the lies that are whispered in our ears. The lies that tell us that we are not as good as the other person. We are not as attractive as others. We are not as talented as others. We are not this and we are not that. We concentrate on these things when we should be concentrating on who God has created. Something beautiful. Something precious and special.

That confused young man from Sydney still hears those voices speaking into his ears telling him that he is out of his depth. Telling him that he does not know as much as he should. Telling him that he has no right to be trying to teach other people. And much more. But now that young man has matured into someone different and he chooses to shut out those lies and rather believe that He is in the place where God wants Him, doing the things that God has trained and equipped him for. He looks back down that road and sees classroom after classroom where God has changed his thinking and beliefs. And all along that road he sees that God has walked with him. He now sees other classrooms full of students that he is teaching. Teaching them some of the things he has learned about this amazing God and hoping that they too will see their lives changed for the better. That they too may go out and reach the broken and lost as they reach under the veneer which this world covers itself with and find the broken and hurting people who they can bring to a message of hope. A message about a God who cares. A God who loves them so much that He paid a great price for their lives. A God like no other.

I could not have imagined in my wildest dreams what my life has turned out like. I am so thankful for this great adventure like no other. I am so thankful to know the God who is so faithful. So merciful. So trustworthy. The God who speaks to people if they deign to humble themselves and listen. The God who loves with a love that is indescribable. The God who reaches out to all of us that we might know ourselves as He knows us.

I grew up knowing and believing that there is a God. My understanding then was that God was elsewhere. He seemed distant and unreachable because I could not be good enough to interact with Him. I have now come to a place where I believe this God is with me all the time, as He promised to be. I can say, with Job, that *"I had heard of Him by the hearing of the ear, but now I see Him."*

I have come to believe that God is not just focussed on us as the pinnacle of His creation but that His *"intent"* is toward us. He has our highest good in His heart. His focus on us is not just a casual thing. He intentionally works for our good. As we seek His will and choose to live in His kingdom, we can be sure that His intention is towards us and His blessing is on us.

I hope that this book might have inspired you to seek God more earnestly. To desire to know more of His character. To learn that walking with Him is an adventure like no other.

Appendix 1
Hearing God's voice

Through this book I have mentioned a number of times that we had heard God speaking to us or leading us. I know for many people this would seem a strange thing. It was a strange thing for me all those years ago when I heard people talking like that. What on earth did they mean?

History has many stories of people who claim to have heard God speak to them. The so-called Mad Monk, Rasputin, in Russia was one. Nostradamus is another. In more modern times we have seen the devastation caused by people such as Jim Jones who led thousands of people to their death in South America. I even recall my father telling me about a man in Sydney, Australia, in the early part of the twentieth century who declared that he had been told by God that Jesus was going to return to earth and would walk on the water as he passed through the headlands of Sydney harbor. This man had sold hundreds of tickets to the event, which of course never happened.

So, when someone like myself says they have heard God speaking to them, is it just a sign that I am going crazy? A valid question I believe. I believe that history also shows us that God does speak to His people. Of course, in reading the Bible we read many times where God speaks to His people. But if we continue through history, we can find wonderful examples of the same thing. Was Martin Luther following the guidance of God when he challenged the teaching of the Catholic Church of the day? A challenge that went on to lead to what we call the reformation. Were John and Charles Wesley hearing God lead them through the amazing revivals they saw in the UK? Did William Wilberforce achieve what he achieved with the abolition of slavery because he followed the voice of God? I would say a resounding yes, yes, and yes. And there are many other examples I could add to this short list.

So, what do I mean when I say God spoke to me? For me I have never heard an audible voice from heaven. No flashing lights. No shining angels. No heavenly chorus. In fact, in some ways a little more boring ways. I guess the best way to explain this is to just relate what we have seen and heard.

Probably the first time I can recall anything like this was just a few months after becoming a believer in Melbourne. The church was running an outreach to the people of St Kilda. We had the coffee shop operating but each day we would go to the streets, or the local beaches and talk to people about faith. One such occasion I was teamed up with an older Christian guy and we got into conversation with a couple of young guys. As my friend was talking, I had this strong sense that one of these guys was using drugs. When I say a strong sense, I mean it was not just a thought. It was a very strong impression and the word "drugs" was almost what I was seeing. In the middle of the conversation, I burst in and said, **"What drugs are you doing?"** The look on their faces said so much. One of them had a look of shock on his face and finally he said, **"How did you know?"** These guys showed no outward signs of being regular street users. They just looked like pretty average young men. That statement led us into a long conversation about God being so concerned for them that He had spoken to us and told us something about them.

A few months later when I was praying about whether I should join the team going to Britain I had a strong impression of a particular Bible verse that came to my mind. Bear in mind that I was not any

Appendix 1 Hearing God's voice

sort of biblical scholar at this stage, and probably still am not. I was asking God for direction on whether I should join this team or not. The verse that came was from the book of Isaiah, chapter 6, verse 8. It says, *"Then I heard the voice of the Lord, saying, 'Whom shall I send, and who will go for us?' Then I said, 'Here am I. Send me!'"* Fairly clear I thought.

In other circumstances God's leading has been a thought that grows over time. In situations like that, if I feel that the thought is something that God is saying, I will then talk to my wife about it. Then we will pray about it and ask God for some form of confirmation. Depending on what we think God is saying we may then go and talk to someone who we see as having spiritual authority, or they may be someone in a leadership position in our lives. God speaks to people in many, many ways. We are hearing testimonies now of many people in the Muslim world having dreams of Jesus. These are not just one or two people, but it seems many, many people are finding the true God through dreams.

One of the unique things about the God we follow is that He desires to communicate with us. No other being that professes to be a God is like this. Most are distant, unreachable beings that if they do deign to speak it is only to a special few. The God of the Bible reaches out to speak to all. He does not wait for us to be perfect, which we cannot be. He desires to speak to you too. Put yourself in a position to hear, and you will.

Appendix 2

Provision

As you have read through this book you may have a lot of questions about "how did they afford to do all this?" A fair question. Just as I believe that God speaks to us, I also believe that He provides for us as we walk the road He has directed for us. That last bit is the key part. Being in the place where God wants us.

I preached a sermon once called *"Are you going somewhere with God, or is God going somewhere with you?"* It may sound like I was just playing with words, but the question is really about who is in control in your life? I believe it is a valid question for everyone who is a believer. Most people grow up and at some point, we begin to think about what we want to do with the rest of our lives after we finish school. In fact, in most education systems students are encouraged to think seriously about their future so that they can choose appropriate subjects to follow at school. There is nothing wrong with this process. However, it seems to me that when we become believers in Jesus all things change. The road that we were heading down, indeed the road that we had been focused on for so long, may well be a different road to the one God has for us. You see, when we are young quite often the road ahead can be influenced, and decided in fact, by many other factors. Not least, the influence of our families. Once again, I revert to history here. Biblical history is rife with examples of people who were heading down a road that they, or their families, had set for them until God stepped in. In the Old Testament we can think of Joseph, Moses, Gideon, and David. When we move into the New Testament, we can read about Jesus calling His disciples. Fishermen and tax collectors, to walk away from their trade or business and follow Him. Never going back to what they knew. The Apostle Paul, who was set for a life as a Jewish scholar, ends up as a teacher and preacher for a faith that he had previously persecuted. And again, we could walk through the annals of history to name many others. My point being that we may not all be on the road that God wants us on, even though we are providing for our families and being good citizens, etc. Did we ever ask God what we should be doing? How would He want us to use the gifts and abilities that He gave us? It is indeed a crucial question, and certainly when it comes to His provision.

For us, we have seen God provide in many different ways on our journey, but I have to say that it is really only in the past 10 years that I have been in a place where I have handed over the role of provision to Him. Prior to that time, God in His graciousness watched me try to raise funds for our work, something which I was never very good at I must say. And all through those times He would step in and bring provision from unexpected places and in unexpected ways. He has also used provision, or lack of it, to gain our attention at times or to teach us something new. On many occasions I felt that His timing was far from perfect, but these are times where we continue in faith. Much more could be written about God's provision for different people. Suffice to say that I can only testify to what we have seen and experienced and that is that God is faithful to His word and He does not let us down.

God's provision is not just about finances. We have seen God provide housing, vehicles, employment, education, and much more. It is not just about finances; it is about learning to have a total dependence on God. The more we learn about His character and that He is faithful. He is committed to us. That He has a heart always working for our good, the more we are able to place our dependence on Him. He will not fail us. He is more committed to us than we know. Do we have to step out into what we call full-time ministry to learn this? No. We can learn dependence on God wherever we are. In my early days as a believer, I was aware of a married couple in our church who would sit down each week with the week's pay and they would then ask God what they should do with that money. Sometimes they felt that they should give it all to some need that God directed them toward. Sometimes they simply put it in the bank to use for their own needs. This was placing their dependence on God, not their paid employment. We have to take our eyes off the finances and place them on God. After all, this is what Jesus taught us.

Appendix 3
A few words on addictions

Addictions impact all our lives in one way or another. It is estimated that for every person addicted to drugs or alcohol that another 20 people are affected by that person's addiction. I happen to believe that this figure is grossly underestimated. If we consider that one addict's behavior impacts their immediate family, then their wider family of aunts, uncles, cousins, and grandparents. Add to this work colleagues and friends and then add law-enforcement officers, court officials and prison officers. We can quickly arrive at a number well in excess of 20 people affected by one addict.

If we look at how the broader community is impacted, we only have to consider increased insurance premiums and other health costs such as HIV and Hepatitis C, both of which are connected to the addiction community. So, although we may think we are not really affected by addictions the truth is that we are. It is also important to remember drug and alcohol abuse impacts the road toll numbers, road rage, family violence, and murder rates. In short, I believe that the community needs to understand that addictions are a bigger problem than many of us want to believe, and that problem is growing, according to the United Nations 2019 report on drug use across the world.

Throughout this book I have mentioned several issues that people wishing to deal with drug or alcohol addiction need to face up to. I have also mentioned some of the things that their supporters need to consider as well.

At this point I want to highlight a few issues that people may find helpful, either as someone struggling with addiction or someone facing the trauma of an addiction in their family.

Most people seeking recovery from addiction have an expectation that, if they complete the recovery program, then everything will be different, and they can get on with living life much like everyone else in the community. The truth is quite different. Recovery programs will bring breakthroughs, there is no doubt about that. The longer a person goes without using, the stronger they become. Yes, even in Christian recovery programs we see relapse as a part of recovery. A person with an addiction problem may carry the desire with them for many years after the initial program has ended. Breaking away from life controlling problems is never an overnight event. It is a long road that gets easier each day. But for the readers who do not have an addiction issue can I suggest that you recall any behavioral problem that you have tried to change in your own life. It could be a struggle with telling the truth. It could be a struggle with attraction to the opposite sex. It could be a struggle with a whole host of things. How long did it take you to break it? Do you still have thoughts about it?

Honesty.

People in recovery must learn how to be brutally honest with themselves and others. The addiction has produced in them an ability to lie without realizing it at times. We used to have a saying in Beth Shalom. How do you know when an addict is lying? When their lips are moving. This may sound harsh, but it is true, and the residents at Beth Shalom would laugh because they knew it to be true.

One of the biggest lies that people struggling with drug or alcohol addiction believe is that they can change all on their own. The truth is they cannot. I think nearly every client I have dealt with over the years has said to me, "I don't need to go to rehab, or a 12-step program. I can do this all on my own." Statements such as this are a clear indication that the person has clearly underestimated the enormity of the challenge ahead of them in recovery.

Manipulation.

My experience with drug users is that they are great manipulators. They can do this by lying. By telling you what a wonderful person you are, or by threats. In recovery they need to learn how to deal with tough situations in honesty and humility. Realizing that if someone else disagrees with them that is ok.

Emotional growth.

Drug or alcohol addiction will stunt emotional growth in a person. Most of us grow emotionally by learning how to deal with tough situations in life. When the addict is faced with a crisis they will go and use their drug of choice in the hope that the crisis will have disappeared the next time they look at it. In this process they do not grow emotionally. They then react to situations and people like a child with tantrums. It is difficult for a grown adult to be honest that they are just a little child inside. That they don't know how to deal with problems without anger and threats of violence. This takes humility on their part to learn a new way of dealing with tough situations in life.

Facing outwards.

Addiction is a very self-centered behavior. It is all about "me" feeling good. The actual act of drinking or using drugs is about medicating emotional pain. This need keeps them focused on themselves which eventually means that they think the world revolves around them. In recovery they should learn to focus outside of themselves onto other people's needs before their own.

For any of us when we focus outside of ourselves it is amazing how small our problems become.

They Need Someone Alongside Them.

To get through recovery properly, the addict needs to have someone they are accountable to. Someone who will be honest with them and work to keep them honest, while also respecting them as a person.

There are many other things that addicts need to deal with, but I just wanted to highlight a few of them here. If you know someone in recovery, please understand that they are going through a very tough process of change. None of us like change, but as someone once said, *"Change is here to stay."* For the addict change is tough. It takes them out of their comfort zone. Recovery is about constant change. So, can I encourage the reader to have patience with the person in recovery. Remember that when you have tried to change at times then others have had to put up with you as well.

What can families do?

Since we began working with families, I have come to believe that they are in fact the forgotten people in the broad public debate

Appendix 3 A few words on addictions

about drugs. Governments in many countries have programs in place, however limited, for the drug user. In Melbourne, Australia there are counseling centers for users. There is a needle distribution program for users. There is even a drug injecting room setup for users, complete with full-time medical staff on hand. But what about the families? Without doubt, the family of a drug user, or alcoholic, is in some form of trauma. Most of them are living with varying levels of shame and a sense of failure. Each day has the possibility of bringing some new crisis and yet each day there is a hope that today will be the day when it all changes.

The impact of the user on the family is enormous. They have been lied to. They have been stolen from. They have been abused and, in many cases, assaulted physically. They have been promised by the user on many occasions that it will change only to have their hopes dashed again. Mum and dad are often at odds with each other and if there are any siblings of the user, they are likely to be struggling with issues of their own as they watch their loved sibling sink into a sea of despair. Just as the addict has an impact on the family, the impact of the family of an addict in recovery should not be underestimated.

We encourage families to try to find a support group that they can attend regularly. This is an area that churches could easily jump into. We talk with families about resetting the boundaries in their household that have been torn down. Usually, the drug user or alcoholic has become the center of the family and instead of the family operating in a healthy manner towards each other the addict is in control.

Families can overcome these desperate times. However, they cannot do it on their own. They need support. They need friendship. They need you. They need Jesus. To assist a family in this situation you do not need to be a drug counselor. You just need to be a friend. Stay in touch with them. Have a coffee with them. Invite them to events. Include them.

Addiction is wider and deeper than you may think.

Addictions are not just related to drugs and alcohol. One addiction that I will mention that has crept up on society, and is now of immense proportions, is pornography. In the church particularly church leaders are recognizing just how dangerous this addiction has become. One church leader I spoke to told me that this is a major problem, and growing, and it is not just men involved. Women are just as likely to be addicted as men. I highlight this addiction in the church because I want to alert the church to the problem in their midst and appeal for church leaders to recognize this and plan for ways to start to address the problem.

Books.

Below is a list of books by some of the people mentioned in this book. It is not an exhaustive list, but I have included books that have had an impact on myself. I hope you may read and enjoy them and be as challenged as I was.

Loren Cunningham: *Is That Really You Lord?*

The Book that Transforms Nations

End Bible Poverty

Daring to Live on the Edge

Winkie Pratney: *Youth Aflame*

Doorways to Discipleship

The Nature & Character of God

Revival. Principles to Change the World

Devil Take the Youngest

Corrie Ten Boom: *The Hiding Place*

Tramp for the Lord

In My Father's House

Prison Letters

Brother Andrew: *God's Smuggler*

Secret Believers

No Guts, No Glory

Light Force

Joy Dawson: *Intercession*

Intimate Friendship with God

Knowing God

All Heaven Will Break Loose

Floyd McClung: *Living on The Devil's Doorstep*

I see an Army

Learning to love People You Don't Like

Basic Discipleship

Harry Conn: *Four Trojan Horses*

Contact Information

If the reader wishes to contact the author, please email Warwick at:

warwick@isaacasia.org

For more information about ISAAC International, please visit:

www.isaac-international.org

www.ingramcontent.com/pod-product-compliance
Lightning Source LLC
Chambersburg PA
CBHW021425070526
44577CB00001B/64